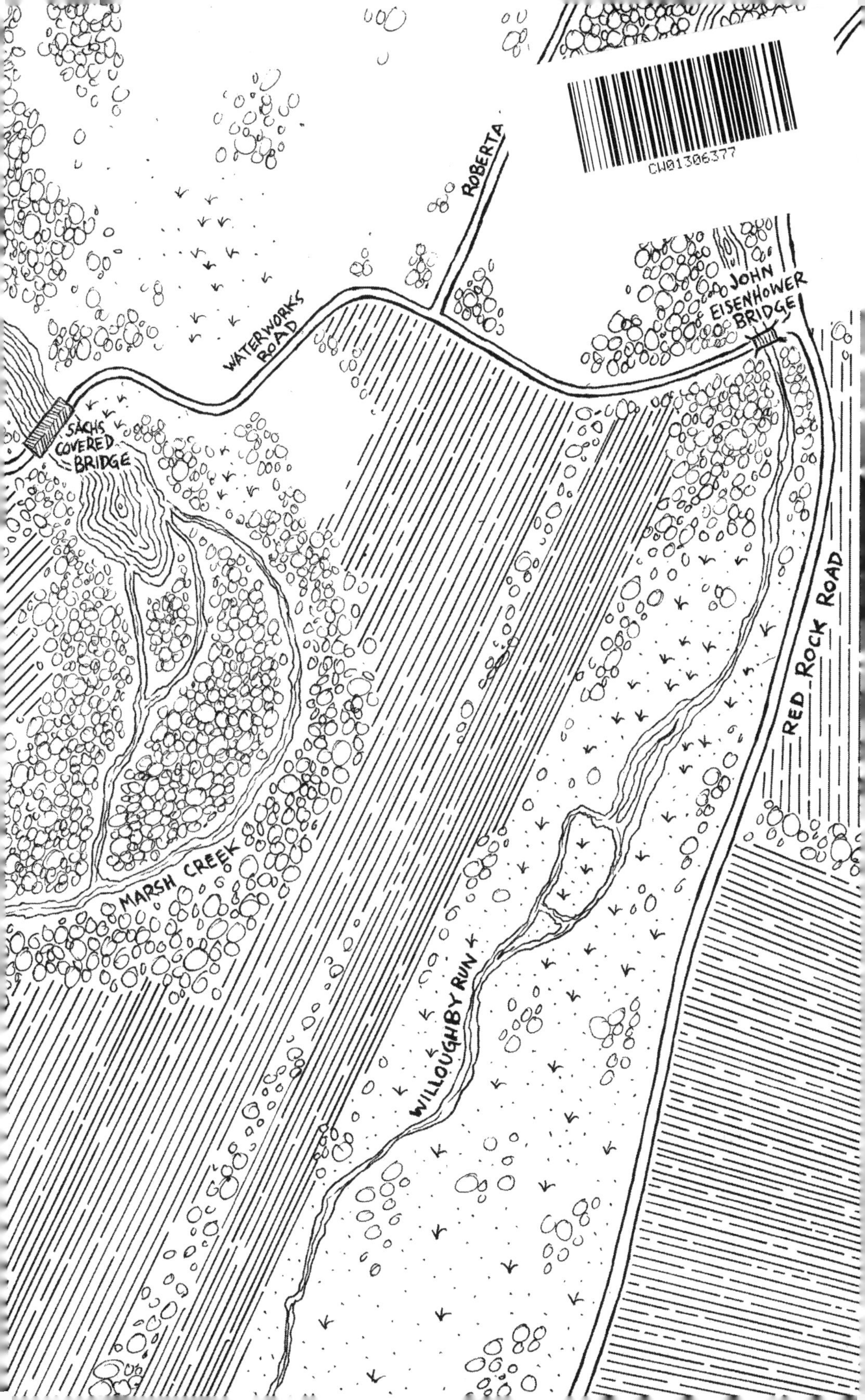
ROBERTA
WATERWORKS ROAD
JOHN EISENHOWER BRIDGE
SACHS COVERED BRIDGE
MARSH CREEK
WILLOUGHBY RUN
RED ROCK ROAD
CW01306377

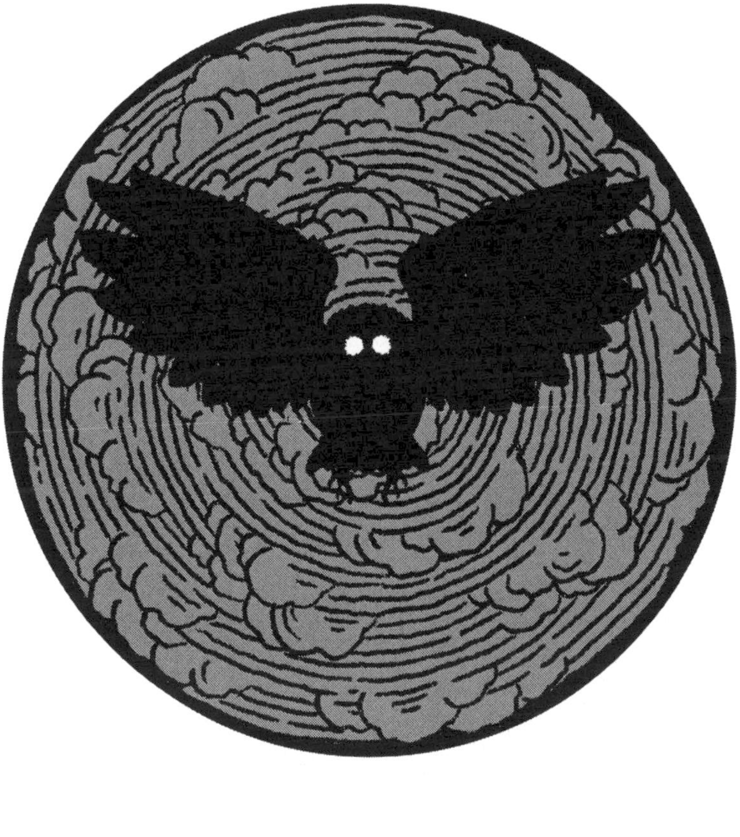

the Witch Cloud

The Haunted Bridges of Gettysburg, Pennsylvania

written, illustrated, and designed by
Timothy Renner

with
Chad Redding
(research collaboration and photographs)

THE WITCH CLOUD

Second Edition 2022.
Copyright © 2021/2022 by Timothy Renner.
Published by Dark Holler Arts / Strange Familiars
StrangeFamiliars.com

All rights reserved.

ISBN: 9798423245023

Dedication

To Chad, who was beside me every step.

The Witch Cloud

· Acknowledgements · Foreword ·
· Introduction: The Other · Rings Around Me ·
· The Iron Bridge · The Wooden Bridge ·
· Creeks and Liminal Spans · Suicide Bridge ·
· First Night · A Weird Web ·
· Buried Treasure Theory · Second Night ·
· The Witch Cloud · Boundaries · Third Night ·
· The Ritual That Never Was · Fourth Night ·
· Confirmation · The Mystery Unsolved ·
· Appendix: The Haunted Bridge on Solomon Road ·
· Afterword · Bibliography ·
· About the Author ·

Acknowledgements

Edited by Catherine Diehl.

Foreword by Alison Renner.

Cover illustration by
Timothy Renner -coloring by Jesse Heagy.

Thank you to Strange Familiars patrons.

Foreword
by Alison Renner

Watch a drop of blood in a glass. It floats and weaves in an unpredictable course, finally surrendering to the same substance in which it is primarily composed. Blood is dripping in the Summer sun of 1863, weaving its way into the darkest of landscapes. The course is unpredictable, but as it returns to the Earth, the blood takes with it the hopes and fears of nearly 50,000 men. The soil acts as a sponge for lost youth, impossible fear and pain.

Gettysburg is unequipped for the carnage, unequipped for the smell, the bodies, the blood. What town is equipped to deal with hell when it arrives at its doorstep? Much of the work of burying bodies falls upon the small African American population of the town. The government supplies the pine coffins. Residents carry peppermint oil to help quell the stench of death. A nation dons black clothes for what seems like an eon.

By 1895 the smell has subsided. A generation has reached adulthood within the confines of the gilded age, never having personally known the horror of the Civil War. The Gettysburg Battlefield is officially established this year, though veterans, opportunists, historians and nostalgia seekers have been returning to the site since the day the soldiers marched onward.

An accidental economy grows in the places where bodies once lay. Monuments dot the landscape. Sunday picnics are held on the green grassy hills where young men drew their last breath. In the soil beneath a picnic blanket, bones are moving. The March rains have displaced the dirt, mud is giving up its contents. Soon, a small portion of a person will reach the surface. Will this bone be found, respectfully returned to the Earth? Will this shard be unknowingly crushed under a mower or reside under leaves for a few seasons? Will the mud submerge it again?

If the soil purges its contents in a cyclical fashion, what does the aether do? Do the layers of emotion, memory and "energy" expel their inhabitants in a similar fashion? Does a collective memory remain still and undisturbed until seekers kick the dust around the

Other? Watch a drop of remembrance as it bobs and weaves its way through the aether, finally surrendering to the same substance in which it is primarily composed.

Introduction: The Other

This is a book about haunted bridges. I would ask the reader, however, to expand their idea of what *haunted* can mean. The paranormal is, in this author's experience, a spiderweb. Where you find ghosts, you often find mystery lights (UFOs). Where you find mystery lights, you often find cryptid creatures like bigfoot. Where you find bigfoot, you often find poltergeist activity.

While many ghost hunters often want nothing to do with bigfoot researchers and most UFO enthusiasts would prefer to be rid of any associations with ghosts or cryptids, the uncomfortable truth is, if you pull hard enough on one strand of the paranormal web, you will find yourself tugging at the other strands as well.

It isn't a nice, neat web. It is tangled and messy and difficult to comprehend, when we can make any sense of it at all.

I attended a ghost hunt in a cemetery one night. I spoke at some length with one of the investigators about his techniques which involved capturing ghost fingerprints on mirrors and leaving talcum powder on the floor to see ghost footprints. As someone who spends most of his "paranormal time" in the woods, these ideas excited me.

I told the ghost hunter, "We are doing the same thing! You are looking for ghost footprints in powder while I am seeking bigfoot prints in mud." He looked at me, confused, unable to see the connection.

We both carry audio recorders, hoping to capture vocalizations from the unknown. Bigfoot and ghosts both go "bump" in the night—issuing various knocks, raps, and slaps. If one explores the stranger side of bigfoot reports, the creatures become even more ghost-like as they glow, disappear, walk through structures, and generally behave more like a spectre than an undiscovered ape.

It is worth stepping back for a broader view of the paranormal in order to see these connections. Are ghosts and bigfoot the same thing? I don't know. However, no one else knows either, despite what they may claim. I do know, however, that ghosts and bigfoot (and faeries, and "aliens", and the rest of the supernatural host) certainly behave in very similar ways, according to witness reports. For this reason, I refer to the entire phenomena of the paranormal, and whatever may be behind it, as *The Other*.

Rings Around Me

"You're the one... rings around me."

The words were spoken in Chad's voice, but it wasn't Chad talking.

We were standing on an old iron bridge, using a "Ghost Box"—essentially a radio which continuously scans through the channels. The random words picked up by the listener are often attributed to ghosts or spirits using the device to communicate. Of course, it's highly controversial—with many of the more skeptically minded arguing that listeners are making more of what they hear than what it is: simple random words.

Others argue that it isn't the ghost or spirits using the Ghost Box, but that the listeners themselves are influencing the results: essentially, one is communicating with one's own subconscious. (To which I would reply: this is just as interesting and important as communicating with some Other spirit).

Whatever Ghost Boxes may be—however they work—those words: "You're the one ...rings around me" brought with them an immediate and striking vision. I saw myself, clearly, drawing a magic circle on the bridge, burning offerings, and attempting to manifest this spirit—or whatever it was—within the circle.

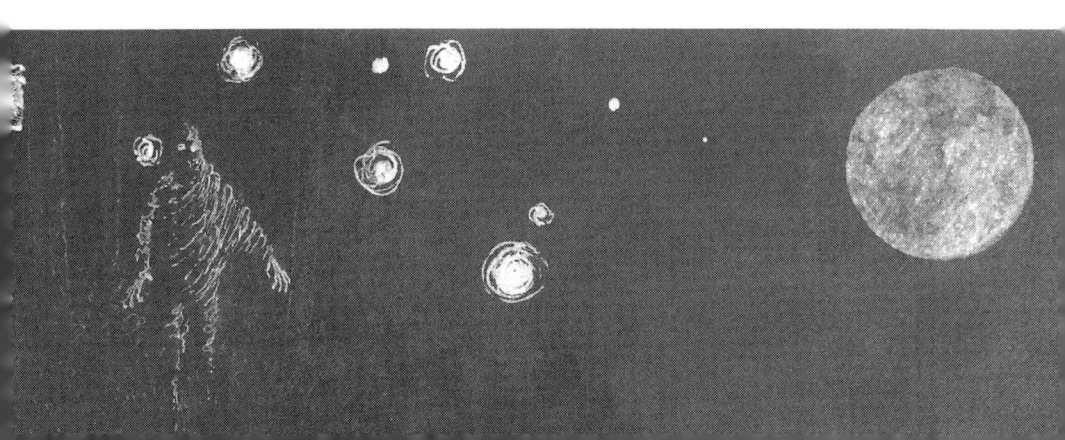

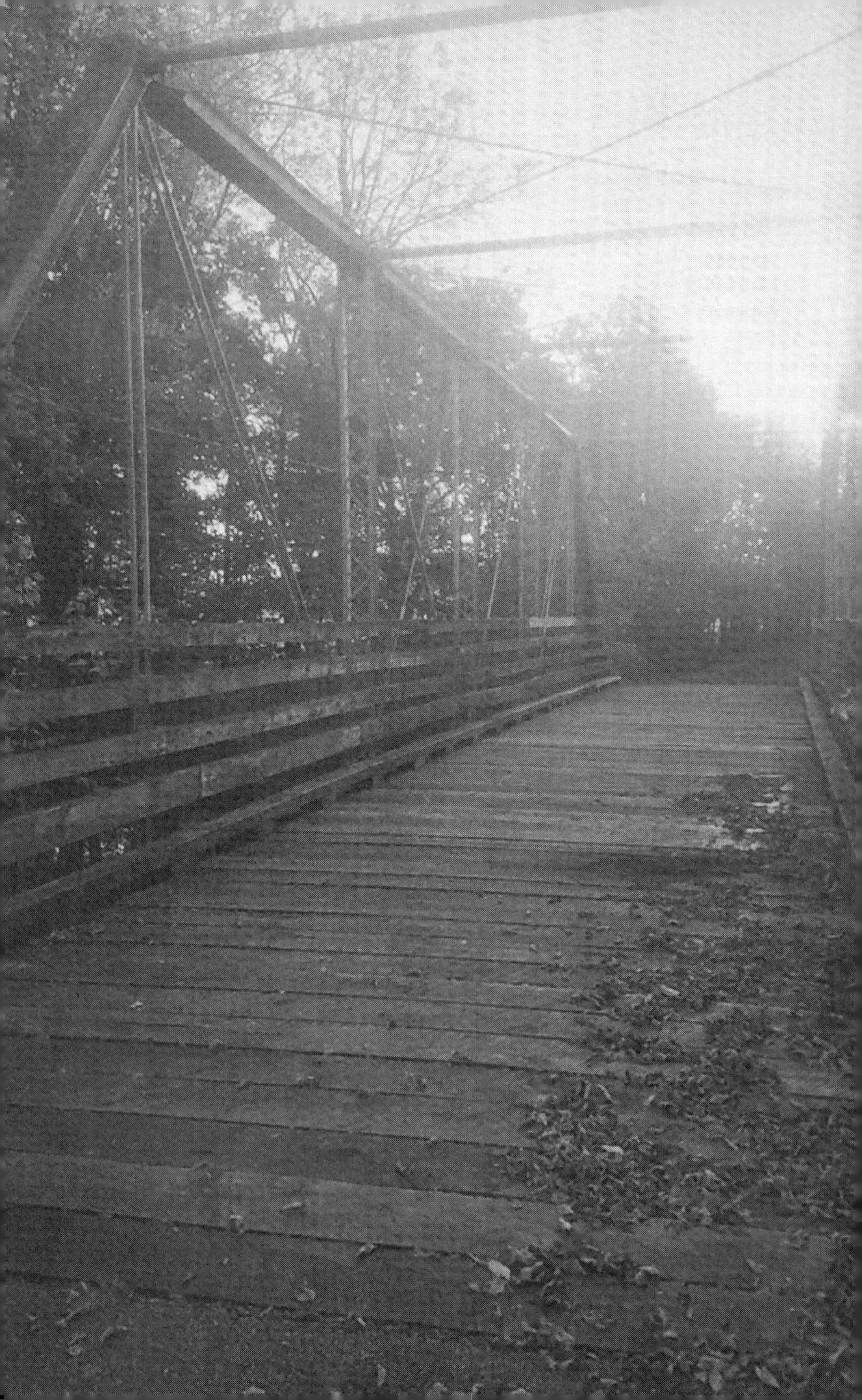

the Iron Bridge

John Eisenhower Bridge crosses Willoughby Run creek just west of the National Park/battlefields in Gettysburg, Pennsylvania. Now closed to traffic, this single-span wrought iron bridge was built in 1886—two decades after the end of the Civil War. As haunted sites in Gettysburg go, Eisenhower Bridge is one of the very few locations that isn't associated with the great and bloody battle at Gettysburg.

If you're looking for Eisenhower Bridge, you might ask the locals instead for *Suicide Bridge*. If you meet local people on the bridge and ask them about the name, they will tell you stories of a person—or *people*—who hanged themselves from the bridge, thus earning it the gruesome title.

The problem with these stories is no one can seem to put a name or a date to them. They are spoken as a known fact, yet I have found no newspaper articles or other documentation to suggest this hanging—or hangings—ever happened. Without a name or a date, it may be impossible to determine if any suicides actually happened on Suicide Bridge.

I've debunked urban legends before. A good portion of my first book, *Beyond the Seventh Gate*, was spent revealing the truth behind the outrageous (and false) legends of insane asylums, mad doctors, and supposed gates to Hell located on York County's infamous Toad Road. And yet, Toad Road and the area around it, is filled with strange encounters, ghosts, cryptids, and more.

I suspected Eisenhower Bridge is the same sort of place. There probably weren't any suicides on that bridge—just like there wasn't a mad doctor experimenting on hapless patients along Toad Road. The question remains whether people crafted the tales of suicides to explain the weirdness that already existed around the bridge—or, instead, was the weirdness somehow *drawn* to the bridge by legend-tripping ghost hunters simply believing that something dark had occurred there?

There are some tragedies and other strange stories associated with the Eisenhower Bridge and surrounding areas, before the iron span was closed to traffic.

- Though the bridge wasn't erected until after the Civil War, the area did see fighting during the Battle of Gettysburg. An article on the fighting published in the *Gettysburg Compiler* in 1899 noted that Willoughby Run was "crimsoned by the blood of brave men."

- In the summer of 1910 a group of what the papers termed "gypsies" took up temporary residence in the fields around Willoughby Run. While "gypsy" is now frowned upon—and the preferred term is the correct *Romani* when referring to said people—there is also a problem with articles in old newspapers referring to any groups of traveling people as "gypsies", no matter their heritage. So, while it is likely that the "gypsies" in question were Romani people, we cannot be sure when looking back.

    This group of traveling people, whatever their heritage, was initially taken into custody by the sheriff but, upon paying for a permit, were allowed to stay in their camp along the creek. The permit gave the group of 30 and their six wagons the right to stay along Willoughby Run for the remainder of the year. The papers noted that the group was telling fortunes and only intended to stay in Gettysburg until they made back the costs of the permit and associated fines.

- In 1916, Alexander Spriggs, a farmer who lived along Willoughby Run, awoke to find his cow had been cruelly attacked overnight. Someone had made five vicious cuts into the bovine. The cow was so severely injured that it had to be killed. The attack was thought to have been the work of an insane man, Harvey Hansford, who was, afterward, taken to an asylum.

- On June 18, 1919 a young boy was the victim of an attempted robbery just after crossing the bridge. The eleven-year-old boy was transporting a crate of eggs by horseback. The would-be-robber jumped out and attempted to grab the reins, but the horse was frightened and took off at a wild gallop. The boy was not injured, but the entire crate of eggs was broken.

- In 1921 a young man accidentally ran his horse into the stone wingwall leading to the bridge. The animal suffered an injury to its back and had to be put down on the bridge.

- On July 1, 1985, a 49-year-old man flipped his pickup truck into Willoughby Run, near Eisenhower Bridge. He died from injuries sustained in the crash. July 1 is an interesting date, as that day in 1863 marked the first day of fighting in the Battle of Gettysburg.

    Willoughby Run, red with soldier's blood; fortune tellers encamped on the banks of the creek; tragic animal deaths; attempted robberies—these were simply a sampling of the more interesting oddities which happened on and around the bridge. A number of other auto accidents happened in the area—one logging truck broke the planks on the iron bridge, only kept from the creek below by the iron supports underneath.
    Another vehicle overturned, leaving bodies of men strewn about the scene. When rescuers arrived, they believed all of the accident victims dead until they realized that they were simply drunk on hard cider and passed out. One of the victims, semi-conscious, noted a man came upon the scene previous to their rescuers, saw the carnage and, rather than help, simply picked up one of their jugs of hard cider and left the scene.
    One of the strangest and most surprising things found in our

research was a kind of personal synchronicity. The iron bridge was officially named John Eisenhower Bridge in the 1960s—sometime after President Eisenhower moved to a farm in the area following his term in office. However, before this the structure was sometimes known as *Redding's Bridge*.

A family in the immediate area of the bridge bore the surname *Redding*. In fact, the property on which the Eisenhower Farm was built was purchased from the Redding family. Chad's last name happens to be Redding.

Before we found this out, Chad, of the two of us, already seemed to be more connected to—*and affected by*—the area. When we would detect cold spots, or even just note that *eerie* feeling that seems to precede weirder activity at haunted places, it was almost always Chad that noted these things first.

Whatever *Other* things inhabit the area of the iron bridge seemed to be haunting Chad as much as the span itself. It was as if he carried away something with him after each of our visits. Often this took the form of Chad being sick or exhausted the following day. One morning, following one of our excursions to Eisenhower Bridge, Chad had an appointment at the Adams County government offices. To his surprise, hanging on the wall in the office was a large, framed photograph of the iron bridge. "I can't seem to get away from this place," Chad told me.

Chad and I both began to wonder if he didn't have some familial connection to the land itself. There aren't many Reddings in the area. Even if he is not related to the Gettysburg Reddings, it is still a rather amazing synchronicity. What are the chances?

the Wooden Bridge

About a half mile to the west of John Eisenhower Bridge is a more famous bridge, a structure that spans Marsh Creek (Willoughby Run is a tributary of Marsh Creek). This is the famous Sachs Covered Bridge,

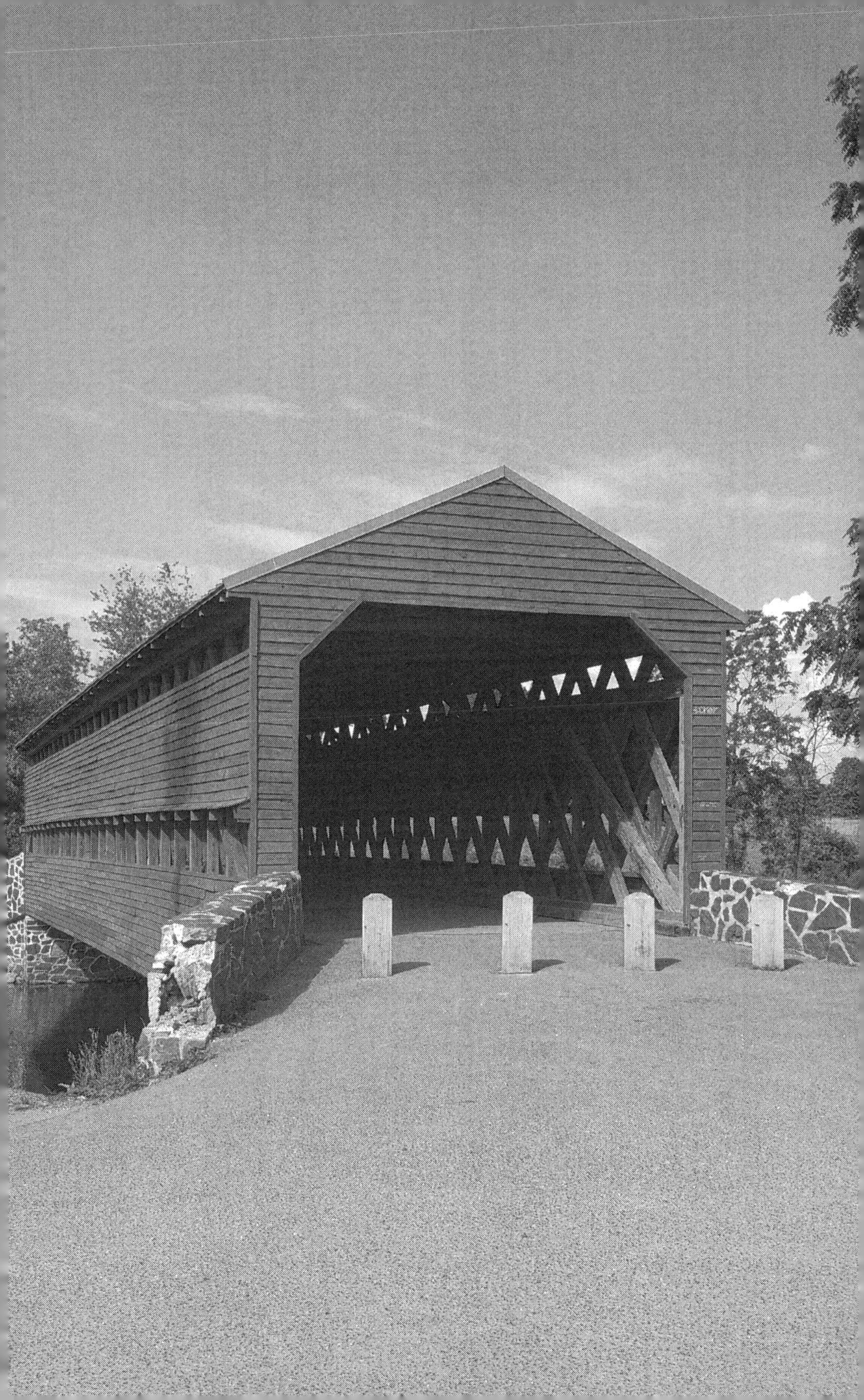

which has been featured prominently in various TV programs, books, and websites dealing with the haunted sites of Gettysburg.

Eisenhower Bridge and Sachs Bridge are connected by a path—once a road, now closed to automobile traffic—that starts at Red Rock Road, crosses Eisenhower Bridge, and passes through a very small yet very dark stand of woods before it opens up to farm fields and houses. Eventually this path turns into Waterworks Road. Following Waterworks Road west will lead you directly to Sachs Bridge.

Sachs Bridge, unlike Eisenhower Bridge, did exist at the time of the Civil War—it was built in 1852—and was used both by Union and Confederate troops to traverse Marsh Creek. While closed to traffic today, pedestrians can still walk or ride bicycles across the span, enjoying the atmosphere of the covered bridge and the grand views it provides of Marsh Creek and the surrounding area.

However, despite its rural charms, Sachs Bridge is not without its historical darkness. Besides its general association with the bloody Battle of Gettysburg, legend holds that three men, Confederate deserters, were ordered to be hanged from the beams of the bridge by General Longstreet. The corpses of these men were left swinging by their necks—a horrid warning for any other would-be-deserters.

Conflation happens frequently in folklore. Especially when the geographic locations of two or more stories are close to each other. Stories—or parts of stories—once initially associated with one location get subtly changed and moved to another. It is somewhat to be expected in the great game of "whispering down the lane" that is folklore. As stories are passed down—often half-remembered—from one generation to another, details are lost, mutated, or combined with other half-remembered stories. With this in mind, I wonder if the supposed suicides that happened on Eisenhower Bridge were not simply someone remembering the story of the hangings on the nearby Sachs Bridge and attributing them, instead, to the iron bridge?

When it comes to ghost stories, there is no shortage attributed to Sachs Bridge. Among spectral lights and the sound of horses galloping across the wooden structure, people have also witnessed disembodied floating heads, the phantom forms of the hanged soldiers, taps on the shoulder by unseen hands, and the sounds of gunfire and cannons echoing from the surrounding woods.

Chad had his own experience on Sachs Bridge, long before we ever met. Chad told the story to me one night while we sat in

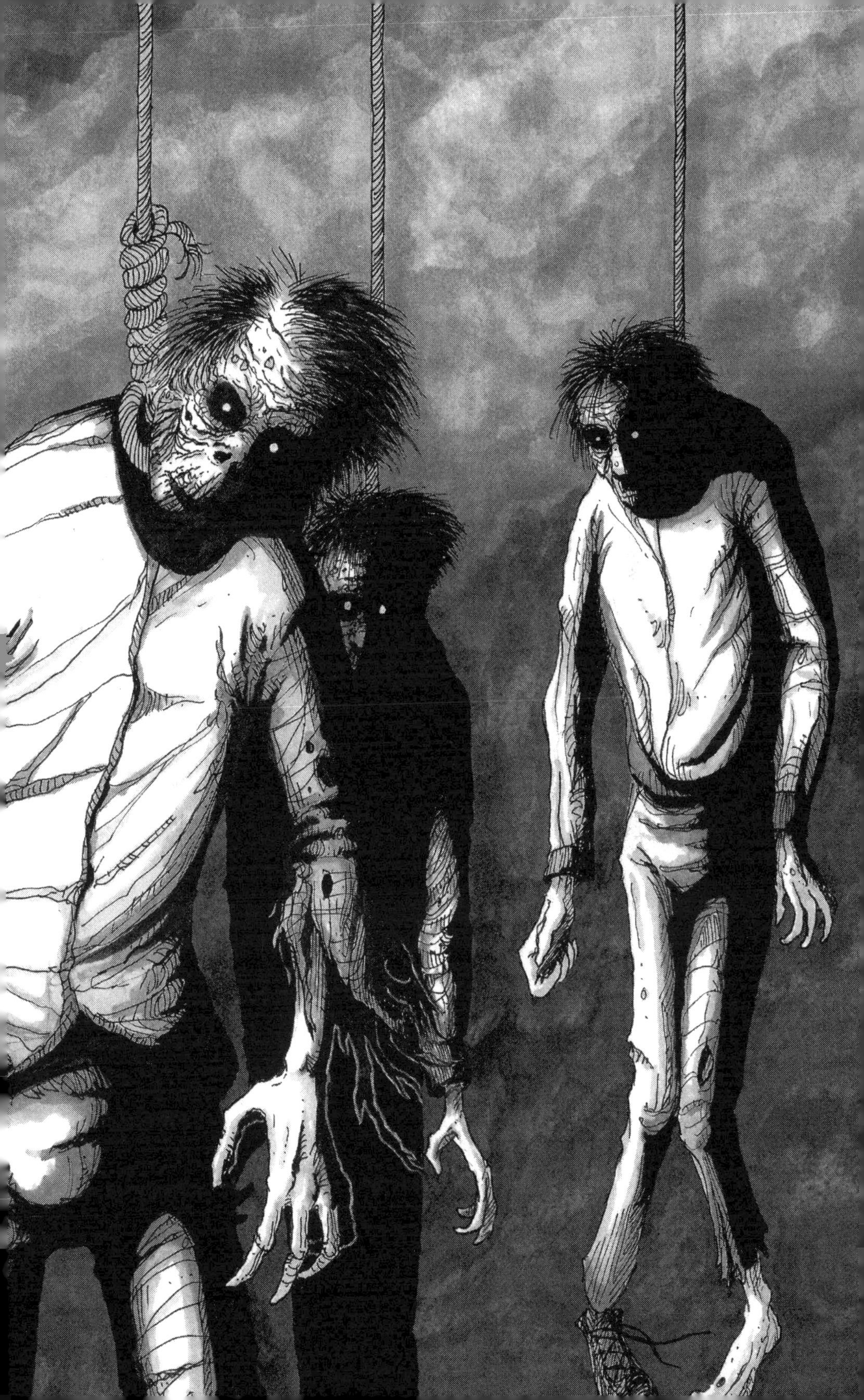

darkness beside the old covered bridge:

> This was 15 years ago...I used to work at a glass factory that's outside of Gettysburg. I worked third shift. I always read about Sachs Bridge but I never really went there. So I was just like, "Oh, I'll just go find this bridge" one morning—because I would get off work—I wasn't really tired. So, I just decided, well I'm going to come over here to Sachs Bridge one morning.
>
> So, I parked and I got out—and I was the only one here. This is like six o'clock in the morning. The sun has just risen. There's not a soul here. The only thing I heard was a crow cawing. I had a phone that had a recorder on it. So, I just turned the phone on to record—just in case something happened.
>
> So, I'm walking across the bridge and as I'm walking I hear a second set of footsteps. I was on this side and as I was crossing—as I got closer to the other side—I just kept feeling weirder and weirder and weirder. A couple times I thought I heard what sounded like footsteps when I wasn't walking. As I got closer to the other end, I would hear what sounded like other footsteps. Then the crow got more excited. It just started cawing more—and I'm just like, "What is going on?" Finally, I just felt cold—I'm like, "Okay it's time to go."
>
> So I started leaving and as I'm walking that's when I heard more [footsteps]——almost like running—coming from that side of the bridge that felt weird....and then I ran. It scared me. [I] didn't see anything—there was nobody here—not a soul. And it wasn't coming from under the bridge.
>
> I got in the car—drove home—and when I was listening to the recorder you could hear—I guess they would be called EVPs*—like voices. You could hear footsteps when I wasn't walking. What was weird was that when the crow would caw—that's when you

would hear the EVPs.

*(EVP or Electronic Voice Phenomenon are unknown voices recorded by audio devices, often during ghost hunts or other paranormal investigations.)

Creeks and Liminal Spans

Two creeks. Two bridges—connected by a road/path that leads directly from one to the other. Two haunted places so close to each other and so similar in so many ways. We began to wonder: was there something more to these hauntings? Was there something about the land between the bridges—between Marsh Creek and Willoughby Run—which, somehow, held onto these dark things and kept them there?

Is there something about bridges which could make them prone to hauntings? Rich Newman, author of *Haunted Bridges*, does not offer a theory as to *why* these structures are host to these phenomena, but as his book collects "over 300 of America's Creepiest Crossings" (as the cover states), we can see there is no shortage of spooky spans.

It's hard to give firm answers when dealing with The Other. I, for one, am not even entirely convinced that what people experience as ghosts are simply the spirits of dead people. As such, I would be careful offering any declarations along the lines of "bridges are haunted because ___."

However, in dealing with the paranormal and all its surrounding uncertainties, I tend to note common factors across supernatural accounts of all sorts. The Gettysburg haunted bridges share two features which grab my attention: they both cross creeks;

and bridges, by their very nature, are liminal places.

In my years as a researcher and documenter of The Other, I have found that, at least in Pennsylvania, strange things seem to follow creeks and rivers. It happens with such regularity that one of the standard questions I ask witnesses to any paranormal event is: Where is the closest creek? Almost always, there is a creek nearby the location of their encounter.

I will allow that part of this may be the geography of Pennsylvania. It seems there are few locations that are not at least somewhat close to a creek. However, the relationship of creeks to the paranormal occurs with such regularity that I often wonder if there is some unknown factor that ties the two together.

Could water running across certain rocks and minerals cause strange images to appear—not unlike magnetic tape passing over the playback head in an audio cassette player or a VCR? Could the very sound of water itself—constantly flowing through the creeks—act in some way like an endlessly chanted mantra, opening unseen gateways to unknown realms?

It is all speculation, of course, but almost every aspect of the supernatural boils down to speculation. Beware the paranormalist who has all the answers.

Liminality is another factor which seems baked into the paranormal experience. Often people experience The Other when their lives are in transition, in one form or another. How often have we heard stories of people on vacation who encountered a cryptid, a UFO, or slept in a haunted hotel room? The stories about families refurbishing their homes and stirring up dormant ghosts or poltergeists are so common as to have almost become a trope in the ghost hunting world.

It would be difficult to find a more liminal structure than a bridge. Bridges are, literally, *in-between*—connecting one stretch of land to another, often spanning dangerous or difficult terrain.

Given their connection to running water and their liminal nature, one wonders if the question should not be "Why are so many bridges haunted?" but, instead, "Why aren't more bridges haunted?"

Suicide Bridge

I first heard the name "Suicide Bridge" at a paranormal conference, far away from Gettysburg, in Scranton, Pennsylvania. I was listening to ghost hunters speak among themselves at the table next to my own. My ears perked up when they mentioned Gettysburg, as I live somewhat close to the town and find myself visiting frequently. One of the ghost hunters declared that Suicide Bridge was by far the scariest site in Gettysburg. Interestingly, she went on to relate a story of visiting and hearing unexplained banging noises issue from the bridge. This is something about which we will hear much more later.

My own first visit to Eisenhower Bridge left me somewhat unimpressed. In October of 2017, I had gone there with Adam Sayne, host of the Conspirinormal Podcast, and my friend James K. who was, at the time, co-hosting Strange Familiars with me.

Admittedly, my approach to the bridge was doubtful and flippant. I had recently published *Beyond the Seventh Gate* and considered myself somewhat immune to these sorts of unprovable local legends. I had already looked for suicides upon said bridge and turned up nothing.

Adam, James, and I arrived at Eisenhower Bridge in the early evening when there was plenty of light left by which to see. Upon seeing the little iron structure, given the reputation that had preceded it, I was somewhat underwhelmed. I boldly called for whatever-was-there to show us what it could do, and made jokes regarding the folkloric name of the place. (These are things which I would not say today!).

We stayed until darkness fell, and experienced nothing unusual. On the way out of the area, however, James had to relieve himself and requested that I let him out of the vehicle. He made his way into some brush as I, jokingly, drove away as if to leave him there. I drove about 100 yards then turned around to retrieve James who was rather unhappy with my little prank. He said as he was urinating the trees and brush began to shake all around him, driving him back out to the road where I found him walking.

While we were on the bridge that night, I did snap several pictures with my phone. Most of the photos showed nothing unusual, however, one—taken after darkness fell—shows what looks to be a tiny light on the bridge. When enlarged, it looks to be a little flame. The light in question is not something shining from the woods beyond (subsequent visits made me quite familiar with the surrounding area—there's nothing in that direction where a light could be). It appears to be in *front* of the ironwork on the bridge.

I am not one for photographic evidence of The Other. In fact, I rarely take photos or videos on our paranormal investigations. They tend to be problematic: controversial and consistently "debunked" by so-called "experts" who "know photography".

I make no such claims. I know very little about photography and, in fact, tend to agree with my friend Tobe Johnson who stated rather eloquently that, in terms of The Other, it is almost like we are *not allowed* to capture it on film. Such are the problems and controversies with paranormal photography. With all of that said, I will present the photograph taken on the bridge in October of 2017 here, as a matter of (hopeful) interest to the reader. You may decide for yourself if it shows something Other, was merely a camera glitch, or is otherwise explainable.

First Night

The first night Chad and I went to Eisenhower Bridge, it was almost as an afterthought. It was August 15, 2020. Earlier in the evening we had been night-hiking through the battlefields and surrounding woods in Gettysburg. As the battlefields close to the public at 10:00 PM, we were looking for another haunted area to explore.

I thought back to my previous visit to Eisenhower Bridge, regretful that I had been so dismissive of the site, and asked Chad if he had ever heard of "Suicide Bridge"/Eisenhower Bridge. While he had, of course, heard of Sachs Bridge, Chad was unaware of the iron bridge. It was a short drive from the battlefield, so I quickly related everything I knew at that time—both truth and legend.

Gettysburg is a tourist destination—not just for history buffs, but also for ghost hunters. There is a "ghost economy" in Gettysburg, fueled by endless volumes of ghost story books describing the various spectres seen in the area and, also, by the many, many ghost tours run by competing local businesses. Between the ghost tours and private ghost hunters, it is not at all unusual to meet up with seekers of the paranormal at all hours.

Such was the case when we arrived at Eisenhower Bridge late that August night. There was a couple on the bridge, Shannon and Bethany, huddled together, looking somewhat shaken. It is a look I recognized—a look I had seen in many other paranormal witnesses. It isn't a look of *fear* exactly, nor is it *confusion* (though both fear and confusion can be part of the mix). It is a look of someone who has experienced something which *should not be* (at least according to mainstream thinking). It is the look many people bear in the wake of

---

previous page: Photograph from the author's first visit to Eisenhower Bridge. The light anomaly is the bright white spot in the middle right of the image.

The Other.
    Bethany and Shannon lived in Gettysburg and had visited the bridge previously, but on this night they had a particularly intense experience. I asked the couple if I could interview them.

> **Shannon:** We were out here earlier and she was sensing a lot. And it sounded like somebody jumped off the bridge onto the ground. [To Bethany]: You want to tell it? Because it happened to you.
>
> **Bethany:** Yeah, so we were here, what, three hours ago? Two hours ago?
>
> **Shannon:** Yeah.
>
> **Bethany:** So, we parked here—and we were literally not even 20 feet off the bridge?
>
> **Shannon:** Yeah.
>
> **Bethany:** And we started hearing...almost like a hammer—but it wasn't really a thick cut like that.
>
> **Shannon:** Yeah, not like a thud like a hammer would make.
>
> **Bethany:** Yeah...
>
> **Timothy:** Did it sound like it was hitting the bridge?
>
> **Bethany:** No, it sounded like it was hitting the sand underneath the bridge... So, then we were walking down that path and I felt a woman's presence. And I closed my eyes and all I could see was a lady wearing white or pale pink. And I started crying.
>
> I said she's not a bad spirit—she's good. She's fine. She's just sad and I feel it. And she stopped me, and I

turned around, and I feel like I hit a cold sheet.

So, then we continued down the path and we hit a spot where it was like: Nope. Nope. No more. We're turning around and going back. And I ran into her again, and I stopped, and I feel like she told me her name was Mary, possibly—but I'm not 100% sure.

Shannon: I've been out to this bridge numerous times—I've had numerous different experiences—and none of them were as in-depth as they were tonight. It was so weird [that] we went home and started researching and this one—I think—video that I had found, like, what we heard tonight is what was in this video. It did—it sounded like somebody...

Bethany: A thud.

Shannon: Yeah, it was a—just—thud!

Bethany: It would sound like a person just... [smacks her hands]

Shannon: Just hit the ground.

Bethany: And we heard it like, what, five times it felt like?

Shannon: Yeah.

Bethany: And then not shortly thereafter we felt—or I felt—her.

Shannon: Yeah, you felt her.

Now, in previous years when I've investigated this bridge, the negative entity that is here is not good. It is not good.

Several things Shannon and Bethany mentioned we would either hear again from other sources, experience ourselves, or both.

The sound of something hitting the earth or the water below the bridge is commonly reported—along with the sound of something hitting or knocking on the bridge itself, as well as sounds of knocks issuing from the nearby woods.

Likewise, the idea that there is a place on the path—not far beyond the bridge—where the road is darkest. This place brings an unsettling feeling to people. It frequently turns people around and, often, drives them away from the area completely. Here too is a cold spot, reported by the couple and many other people as well.

On this warm August night, Chad and I would experience this cold spot for the first time. I have felt these cold areas before, in various haunted places. It is always a strange feeling, but sometimes you are left wondering: perhaps it is a draft or some inconsistency in the building or atmosphere? On this night, however, there was no question: it was the coldest cold spot I have ever experienced. It was like walking into an icebox.

It wasn't cool air rising from the creek or some breeze blowing in from the mountains. You couldn't feel the coldness closer to the creek—or even standing on the bridge, right above the creek. The cold air wasn't moving, like a breeze. It was a stationary spot of frigid air into which you could walk—and then step out again into the warm night.

It was in this area that we saw the first of many strange lights we would witness around the bridge. A subtle, shimmering glow just off the side of the bridge, in the trees.

The more time we spent in the area of that cold spot, the more agitated Chad seemed to get. Eventually, he became nauseous and had to sit down. He felt as though whatever was there—whatever entity or force of The Other—was pulling energy from him. This was the first notion we had that whatever was there could be *vampiric* in nature.

Chad stayed in the area of the cold spot, trying to establish contact with whatever was there—or at least figure out what was making him feel so sick. I returned to the bridge and continued talking with the couple. I had not mentioned what Chad was experiencing in the darkness, some yards down the path, but almost on cue Shannon told me a story of another person vomiting at the location. He described the reaction of Bethany as well: "When she got to the end of the bridge, she was like, 'Oh my God. I feel like I'm going to be sick.'"

Whatever Chad experienced that night left him ill for more than just the time we spent at the bridge. The following day found Chad sick and weary. He was exhausted, with an upset stomach, and had a bad, lingering headache. He spent most of the day in bed. Chad said he simply felt *drained* by the previous night's events and attributed his illness to whatever we experienced at the iron bridge.

Chad offered a theory on the cold spot we experienced. His feeling of being drained was so intense—and that is the word Chad came back to again and again, "drained"—that he wondered if the ambient temperature wasn't changing at all. Instead, he theorized that perhaps we were just feeling colder as whatever-was-there drew energy and health from our bodies.

Later, as I edited the audio Chad and I recorded during our first night at Eisenhower Bridge, two interesting clips caught my attention. Both of these were segments captured on the bridge at a time when the recorder was running, but no one was speaking. They are each brief, but sound, to me, like someone whispering or speaking in a breathy tone. I cannot tell what is being said, if anything—so, I am unsure if it is proper to call them EVPs or simply some unknown audio.

A Weird Web

My second visit to Eisenhower Bridge, and my first with Chad, certainly changed my mind about the location. No longer dismissive and flippant, I was now quite sure that *something* was going on there—but what?

From the first story I heard about "Suicide Bridge" in which the ghost hunters described something unseen banging on the bridge, my interest was piqued. Banging and knocking sounds call, to my mind, cryptids and poltergeists. Bigfoot, it is said, knocks on trees, slaps the sides of houses, and taps on windows. Poltergeists have been known to issue their own variety of knocks, thumps, and bangs.

The connection between bigfoot and poltergeists is explored in some length by my co-author, Joshua Cutchin, in our book *Where the Footprints End: High Strangeness and the Bigfoot Phenomenon, volume I*. In brief Joshua asserted that the "class-B" bigfoot encounter (i.e. an experience where the creature is not actually seen) and poltergeist hauntings hold a lot in common. Both can feature bad smells, unknown language, lithoboly (stone-throwing), and, of course, all manner of bangs and knocking sounds. The similarities led Josh to coin the term *wildnisgeist* (roughly: wilderness spirit) to apply to the poltergeist-like phenomena experienced in the woods.

Because people experienced this activity in the woods, or in areas associated with bigfoot, it has long been assumed that it was bigfoot creatures making the sounds, issuing the bad smells, and/or throwing the stones. However, as the creatures are not seen, perhaps something else is behind the activity. This is where the wildnisgeist theory comes in to play.

Both volumes of *Where the Footprints End* go a long way to point out how often the bigfoot phenomenon is surrounded by other weirdness: ghosts, UFOs, black dogs, faeries, anomalous big cats, witches, mystery lights, other cryptid creatures, etc. When thinking about The Other, I think it is important to look at things from new angles; turn them around; flip them on their heads. Perhaps, as these varied kinds of strangeness surround the bigfoot experience, so the bigfoot phenomenon, perhaps, can creep into hauntings and poltergeist experiences.

In fact Dave W., a friend and previous guest on Strange Familiars, once offered the theory that, perhaps, instead of poltergeist explaining "class-B" bigfoot activity, bigfoot may be responsible for poltergeist activity. This is the kind of thinking that drives crazy those bigfoot enthusiasts who believe the creatures are simple, natural animals or relict hominids. It implies that there is an unseen bigfoot—or an unseen force behind the bigfoot phenomenon. Likewise, it forces the common ghost hunter to consider that there may be more going on in hauntings than the simple lingering spirit of a dead person.

No one *knows*, of course, what is really behind any of these situations. Beware of anyone who gives firm answers as regards The Other. There is a reason all of this activity falls under the heading of *Unexplained Phenomena*. However, my own research and personal experiences have led me to believe that all of this activity—bigfoot, ghosts, UFOs, et al—is somehow related. *How* and *why* it is related, and what exactly is behind it, I cannot say, but there is a reason I refer to all of the phenomena collectively as *The Other*: there seems to be a connective tissue to all types of paranormal encounters.

Ten years ago if someone would have suggested ongoing cryptid activity in the area of Eisenhower Bridge, I would have been extremely doubtful. I would have looked at maps and pointed out that the woods around the bridge are not very deep at all, and there is no nearby wilderness in which the creatures could live and hide.

Nowadays, after years of trying (and failing) to make the "flesh and blood" bigfoot hypothesis work, I see virtually no possibility that a breeding population of giant ape-men could be hiding in Pennsylvania. There is even less of a chance of this population being in south-central Pennsylvania... and yet, bigfoot encounters persist throughout the area. As I believe the many witnesses who have shared their stories with me, I have to wonder then: if they are not seeing an undiscovered animal of some sort, what *are* they seeing? Add to this question all of the other high strangeness that surrounds the bigfoot experience and we arrive at my current *theory*—I hesitate to call it a *conclusion* as I believe there is no end to this quest. This theory is that bigfoot is not a natural creature at all but something *Other*—something which belongs to that same class of phenomena of which ghosts, faeries, and UFOs, are also a part.

Some may accuse me of having "bigfoot on the brain"—which I can not deny. Bigfoot remains my favorite of all the unexplained phenomena. Still, some details of the encounters were whispering "bigfoot" to me. Besides the initial story I heard, of something banging on the bridge, there was James' experience of the brush shaking around him on our 2017 visit.

Shannon and Bethany mentioned the sound of something heavy hitting the ground beneath the bridge. Of course, attributing this sound to bigfoot is a leap worthy of the great ape-man himself, but there are multiple accounts in bigfoot literature of the creatures hitting, slapping, or punching the earth.

A more obscure bigfoot connection was Bethany's mention of a woman-in-white spirit. This was based on her impressions—whether she was psychic, intuitive, or merely *sensitive* I do not know. I wrote an entire chapter in *Where the Footprints End, volume I* which explores the connections of ghostly women-in-white to cryptids, particularly bigfoot. They range from modern sasquatch encounters featuring mysterious weird ladies in white garb to folkloric accounts of European wild men accompanying faerie women wearing white.

Odder yet, I interviewed a witness named Kelly on an early episode of Strange Familiars (episode 15: *Kelly, Don't Pet the Devil Monkey*) who, shortly after encountering a spirit of a woman in white garb at her residence, saw a strange simian cryptid creature on a nearby road. Kelly seemed to be a bit of an intuitive medium herself. She gleaned the name of the woman-in-white at her residence to be *Mary*—coincidentally or not, the same name was attributed to the spirit at the iron bridge by Bethany.

There are, of course, bigfoot encounters documented in Gettysburg despite the lack of wilderness around the town. My book, *Bigfoot in Pennsylvania*, reprints several newspaper articles from 1921 which tell the tale of the "Gettysburg Gorilla"—an unknown, upright-walking, hair-covered creature seen in Gettysburg and the surrounding areas for many months. The "Gettysburg Gorilla" was even in town once—it was shot in a back yard along York Street. (The creature fell after being shot, but got up again and made its way off through the nearby fields.)

The sightings continued through the years. On July 1, 1961 (there's that July 1 date again!), a 13-year-old boy was playing hide and seek behind a fire hall just south of Gettysburg when he backed into a creature. The hominoid was just over 5-feet tall, covered with long hair, and exuded a strong, musky odor.

In 1998, a couple was driving on Route 116, just east of Gettysburg, when they saw a 7-to-8-foot tall creature step over a fence with ease, before crossing the road in just two or three strides. The couple reported that the entity was covered with "longish" black or brown hair and possessed eyes which glowed red, even when not reflecting the car's headlights.

A 9-foot bigfoot creature was witnessed at the Gettysburg KFC restaurant on June 1, 2011. A man on his way to work, around midnight, saw the creature eating food from a KFC bucket removed from the dumpster outside the restaurant.

An interesting detail arises regarding these three more modern bigfoot sightings when viewing them on a map. As marked on the *PA Bigfoot Encounters* Google map, all of these sightings are about three miles or less, as the crow flies, from Eisenhower Bridge. In fact, if one were to draw a triangle connecting the three sightings, the iron bridge sits in the middle of the shape.

All of this isn't to conclude that bigfoot is responsible for whatever is happening at the bridge, but simply to note that there are elements of the bigfoot mystery that seem to be present at the bridge. The Other weaves a weird and sticky web.

Buried Treasure Theory

A common feature I have found in many paranormal accounts is the presence or legend of people digging into the ground at or near the location of many sightings. I call this the *Buried Treasure Theory*—for often we find folkloric accounts of ghosts or faeries guarding buried treasure. However, the idea of "treasure" extends beyond hidden chests of gold and into the idea of anything of value hidden or buried in the ground. Often we find this takes the form of mines, quarries, and even underground caverns in which creatures themselves are said to hide.

The presence of these "buried treasures" so close to so many paranormal encounters has made me wonder if the action of digging into the earth itself has something to do with activating or stirring up the supernatural. In folklore, faeries and the dead are often said to make their homes *inside* the earth. There have been various accounts of *goblins*, *lizard-men*, and UFO bases located in underground cave systems. Often, bigfoot witnesses have claimed the creatures hide in nearby abandoned mines, only to emerge at night.

Gettysburg itself can be seen as one big "buried treasure" for, though it is illegal to do so on the battlefields, artifact hunters have dug into the soil here for decades. Bullets, belt buckles, buttons, and all manner of items forgotten, discarded, or lost upon the battlefields have been exhumed by curious tourist and collector alike.

However, a few miles north of Eisenhower Bridge lies what remains of a stone quarry. Located along Willoughby Run, the appropriately named Willoughby Run Quarry is no longer in operation, but it was a functional quarry at the time of the Battle of Gettysburg. During the fighting, one soldier even fell into the quarry after being struck by a minie ball.

The stone cutters left long ago, but the remnants of the quarry remain. Did their digging, over a century past, turn the eye of The Other to Willoughby Run?

Second Night

Chad and I returned to Eisenhower Bridge on the night of August 26, 2020. It was just after dusk and we were standing on the bridge, discussing what we had learned in the interim about the history of the surrounding area. Suddenly, Chad stopped the conversation to report that he had heard voices.

Hearing voices at the iron bridge is not uncommon, but it poses a problem in determining what the voices are and from where they are issuing. As mentioned previously, there are often people around. Ghost hunters and legend trippers come and go at random times. However, many times you can hear voices in the distance that seem to be coming toward the bridge and yet never arrive. Frequently these voices are accompanied by lights that seem to issue from lanterns or flashlights. Like the voices, the lights never seem to make it to the bridge. Perhaps this is explained by people who have decided to turn around before ever making it to Suicide Bridge—but the voices and the lights that never arrive, together and separately, occur with such frequency at this location that we began to wonder if there was something paranormal happening.

It was while we stood in silence, straining to hear the voices (whoever, or *whatever*, issued these particular voices never arrived at the bridge, by the way), that we heard the first of many knocks, bangs, and thumps coming from the bridge that night. These first knocks, on the recording, are subtle—you must listen closely—but they were plain enough to Chad and me.

Some people have suggested that the knocks heard on

Eisenhower Bridge are due to the structure cooling after a hot day. On August 26, 2020, the daytime temperature in Gettysburg only made it to the mid-80s (Fahrenheit). That night it only cooled to the mid-70s. The temperature difference simply wasn't that great.

Besides this, Eisenhower Bridge is shaded by trees—the sun does not beat down on the bridge all day. We heard the knocks throughout the night, over the course of several hours, well into the early morning of August 27. Likewise the sounds seem to come from all parts of the bridge—the iron, the wooden planks, underneath the structure and, sometimes, even from the woods beyond the bridge.

Chad and I decided to walk to Sachs Bridge and spend some time at the other haunted span. That these two bridges are so close and no one has tried to connect them in any way was a wonder to us. Perhaps it is a failing of paranormal researchers. If all that is happening, in their mind, are the spirits of dead people lingering in the area—and since Eisenhower Bridge was built *after* the Civil War—then how could they be connected? Our more holistic view of The Other, however, requires us to look for the connections.

Even the most well-known ghost story associated with Sachs Bridge—that of the three hanged Confederate soldiers—is likely just a legend. While the story is printed as fact in ghost story books and websites alike, we could find no historical documentation of these hangings. Like so many of the other ghost stories repeated as "fact" in Gettysburg, this one seems to be just a good story someone crafted that, after it had been told enough times, became "known" history.

We have heard ghost hunting groups "talking" (via ghost boxes) with what they believed to be the spirits of the hanged soldiers on the bridge on more than one occasion. Other people have reported seeing apparitions of the hanged men. What of their experiences? What of Chad's own experience on the wooden bridge?

It is not my claim that these witnesses are wrong or mistaken—nor that Sachs Bridge isn't haunted. It is only *what* haunts the bridge that I question. If soldiers were never hanged from Sachs Bridge, yet people see apparitions of hanged soldiers, are they really seeing the spirits of dead people who never actually lived? If no suicides ever happened on Eisenhower Bridge, yet people claim encounters with unsettling entities there, are they making contact with the victims of suicides which never actually happened? It seems to me we should look at these hauntings (and indeed *all* hauntings) through a new lens. Stories are nice, but if people are seeing ghosts of fictional characters—of people that never actually lived—then we need a new definition of what ghosts *are*.

We marched across Sachs Bridge, which is almost always populated with ghost hunters, no matter what time of night, and made our way into the woods along Marsh Creek. The wooden bridge is relatively illuminated and quite safe (barring any supernatural threats). The woods, on the other hand, are very very dark. We would have the woods to ourselves.

Into the dark woods we pressed, the loud voices of people on and around the wooden bridge fading behind us. Before long Chad stopped me, seeing movement ahead of us. It was an owl.

It certainly isn't a terribly unusual thing to encounter an owl in the woods of Pennsylvania, however, we had been encountering quite a few during our recent paranormal research. We record our outings and present some on Strange Familiars. Listeners had noted that, often, before we saw or heard something anomalous, they would hear owl calls on the recordings. We started taking note of this ourselves and, indeed, owls would become a much bigger part of this story going forward.

We made our way out of the woods, back across Sachs Bridge and headed back to Eisenhower Bridge. As we were walking through the darkest part of the path—that same area where the cold spot lingers—we encountered a strong, foul smell. It was not a skunk, nor a dead animal, but seemed to have elements of both of those scents. It seemed to come and go, as if it were carried on wisps of candle smoke, rather than lingering heavily in the air.

Just a few steps later, Chad spotted a red light, just off the side of the path, in the trees. There was something about this light that startled him. This in itself was quite unusual. I have spent a lot of time with Chad in haunted places; in dark forests; in cemeteries at the witching hour; and I can attest that Chad is not easily frightened. We have encountered unusual light phenomena a number of times, including high on a dangerous, rocky ridge at midnight on Winter Solstice—miles away from our vehicle. Never have I heard Chad so affected by mystery lights. He described the light as bright red, like an LED, and about the size of a golf ball. As quickly as he saw it, it disappeared.

We continued onto the bridge, and, to our great surprise, Bethany and Shannon were there once again. Chad immediately asked them if they had seen the red light. They replied that they had, but assumed it was us—until we informed them that it was not.

Shannon and Bethany had come to the bridge a couple times, between our first and second visits, and had some very intense experiences.

> **Shannon:** So we came back, and the one night we came back it was just her and I out here. It was active like you wouldn't believe.
>
> **Bethany:** We couldn't even stay ten minutes.
>
> **Shannon:** We couldn't. It was bad. We were standing at the end of the bridge here and we both are facing this way [on the bridge facing west]. She can feel, I guess the lady that lost the kid here plus whatever bad thing is here. This bush started shaking.
>
> **Timothy:** The one right at the end here?
>
> **Shannon:** On this side, yeah. Right here at the end of the bridge. It started shaking—but it started shaking down low. It was just like an animal being there but it was nothing. And I'm looking and she was like "he's here" and then the whole bush started moving—and we were out. She was like "we gotta go." [The "he" the couple is referring to is what they considered to be the negative spirit or entity in the area of the bridge.]
>
> **Bethany:** Tell him about the other night when we came out. We weren't even here for ten minutes.
>
> **Shannon:** No, no...

Bethany: We weren't even here for ten minutes and he was here in full force. We had the owl going. We had bangs on the bridge.

Shannon: She posted online our experience—didn't say anything about the owl—this is how we found out about it. Somebody was here before and they had investigated and they said if you hear the owl, you need to go. He's pissed, you need to go.

This happened that night. The owl went off and that was it. She turned and she was like, "We gotta go. We have to go. He's pissed." The bridge—holy cow—huge knocks.

[Chad and I explain that we had heard knocks on the bridge earlier that evening.]

Shannon: We just got here not too long ago—

Bethany: —and we've already heard it three times.

Shannon: We're coming down the road here... So, she's intuitive-sensitive and we're not even to the bridge yet and she was like, "He knows we're coming." We pull in—as soon as we pull in—mind you, we're the only ones here—there is this entity walking that way [west, on the other side of the bridge—toward the dark area and the cold spot]—and then it just—it disappeared.

It was at the end of the bridge, on the path—and then just went. It wasn't a quick thing. I physically saw it and then—it left. And I'm like, "Did you see that?" And it wasn't human—because the body was wide, but the arms were long... but there wasn't a bottom and there wasn't a head. That's all you could see.

I can't remember how far down the bend [in the path] is but it was not far and he was gone.

Chad: So, just like a big, burly body?

Shannon: Yes.

Chad: Just the torso with the arms?

Shannon: Yes.

Chad: Were there hands?

Shannon: I didn't see any. I couldn't see the legs.

Chad: Because of brush or because the legs weren't there?

Bethany: We don't know.

Shannon: I can't say it was brush because he was on the path—and I saw the clear torso. It was white...

Chad: Was this bigger than human?

Shannon: Oh my God—he was bigger than me—he was broader than—you two stand together and that's probably the width of it.

Chad: You saw shoulders. How tall were the shoulders?

Shannon: Probably [the height of] your shoulders—but wide. Broader. You two stand shoulder to shoulder—that's about what I'm looking at... Again, you could see long arms. [I] don't remember seeing hands. Definitely no head. Definitely no legs... That was the night we heard the owl. That was the same night that the bush shook—this bush right here... then this whole thing [the bush] starts to shake, and shake bad—and we hear the owl she grabs me and and she said, "We gotta go." And, we were gone.

As the couple finished telling their stories, a very audible knock issued from the bridge beneath us. Upon listening back to the recording, you can hear a first, dominant knock, followed in succession by a quieter knock. This pattern of a louder knock, followed by a quieter knock is present on quite a few of the recordings we captured at the bridge.

Bethany and Shannon left before too long. We noted, again, how often Eisenhower Bridge is visited by people—presumably ghost hunters, legend-trippers, and the like—and yet they almost never stay very long. People will spend hours at Sachs Bridge with all manner of electronic ghost-hunting tools, trying to contact whatever may be there, but when they come to the iron bridge most visitors will leave within ten minutes of arriving.

Chad and I spent a couple more hours at Eisenhower Bridge and the surrounding region that night. As we passed through the dark area on the path I caught sight of something in the fields beyond the trees, south of the path. It was some kind of light. We walked further west on the path in order to get a better view. I wanted to make sure I wasn't seeing the lights of a distant farmhouse. Chad pointed out the farmhouse lights off in the distance. They were not in the same area where I had seen the other light.

As we were scanning across the fields, I saw the mystery light again. It was a pale white orb, floating and bobbing slowly, near the ground, at the tree line. It was subtle—not as bright as the lights from the farmhouse—but it was easy enough to see in the darkness. The orb faded in and out of sight—as if someone was dimming a lantern, then turning the flame up again. It moved west to east for perhaps 15 or 20 seconds before disappearing, then the orb—or another one like it—reappeared in its original position and repeated its journey through the dark fields in a similar fashion. We returned to the bridge and walked down Red Rock Road, trying to get a view of the orb from a different angle, but we wouldn't see it again that night.

We had been hearing knocks and bangs all night—issuing from both the iron bridge and the surrounding woods. At one point, we heard a low, heavy thud coming from beneath the bridge. Could this have been the sound of someone—or something—hitting the ground as Shannon and Bethany described the first night we talked to them?

Finally, Chad and I decided to leave a recorder hidden at Eisenhower Bridge and return after a time to see if we could capture any sounds when we were not present. We drove away and returned about 30 minutes later to retrieve the recorder. We had hidden it on the west side of the bridge, toward the dark part of the path. It had been a long night and we were eager to collect the device and head home.

Chad grabbed the recorder and we crossed the iron bridge for the final time that night when a bang sounded beneath our feet. It was the loudest, most forceful sound we had heard yet coming from the bridge. We could *feel* the vibration in our feet. It felt like we were being escorted out of the area in a very impolite manner. It seemed ominous and was, in fact, quite frightening. We took it as our cue to leave.

We captured this final knock on both of our recorders. The recorder I was holding and the recorder Chad retrieved from its hiding place beside the bridge. Unfortunately, the recordings do not translate the volume and power of this knock. This is the nature of recordings (think of the difference of seeing a rock concert in person versus hearing a recording of a live concert), but at least we captured the sound.

When we listened back to the recorder we had hidden at the bridge we heard more knocks and bangs—of varying loudness and clarity—much like the sounds we had captured throughout our second night at the bridge.

The Witch Cloud

What kind of ghosts manifest as massive entities with long arms, bereft of head or legs? How could there be ghosts of people who never lived? What about Chad's feeling of being *drained*—his sickness after visiting Eisenhower Bridge?

Whatever is happening there, it seems to be something more than what is reported in the ghost stories and urban legends regarding the bridge. There is more than one thing happening in this area. The Other has spun its sticky web across the land between Sachs Covered Bridge and Eisenhower Bridge and all manner of weirdness follows in its wake.

I often look to folklore for help making sense of such things. Our ancestors dealt with The Other in the past—it is hardly new phenomena—and have handed down their knowledge and experiences in the form of folklore. An article by Pennsylvania folklorist Henry W. Shoemaker appeared in the *Altoona Tribune* on March 20, 1939 and described a phenomenon in which multiple paranormal events can happen in the same area: the *Witch Cloud*.

Shoemaker notes:

> Where the "witch cloud" hovers anything may happen, even a spectre elk, a werewolf, or even a *bruchlach*, as the very old Pennsylvania mountain people call a vampire. All of which reminds one of George H. Borrow's deathless description of the *estadea* of Spain. "...The estadea are spirits of the dead who ride upon the haze, bearing candles in their hands."

Perhaps the area around the two bridges is not populated

simply by ghosts (the veracity of whose stories cannot be ascertained), but by something like the Witch Cloud, a kind of paranormal fog which hangs over the region, raining strange and eerie phenomena onto the earth?

Many people talk about being *sensitive* to paranormal phenomena in general, by which they mean, presumably, they can detect it easier and/or determine something about its source easier than those who are less sensitive. I am careful about giving too much credence to these claims for I think it can bestow the idea of a kind of super-power or special knowledge on the people making such claims. Whatever abilities humans have to contact or sense The Other are available to all of us. Perhaps some people have practiced and honed those skills a bit more than others, or, like any other skill (i.e. drawing, music, et al), it is possible some people may have more of a natural talent for one reason or another. As far as special knowledge: I remain firm in my belief that no one really knows what we are dealing with and those who claim they do, need to provide proof.

As mentioned previously, Chad certainly seemed more sensitive to the area around Eisenhower Bridge than I was. He seemed disturbed by the area in ways that I had never seen before, in all of our various paranormal explorations. Does Chad's particular sensitivity lend him any special insight into this region? I don't know. However, for whatever it is worth, Chad started to speak of the phenomenon around the iron bridge as being, "Very old. It was there long before the Civil War." There is, of course, no way to prove this—something which Chad himself recognizes—but it certainly provides another twist to the story, however speculative.

If something like a Witch Cloud lingers in the area between Sachs and Eisenhower bridges, why did it come to that place and why does it stay? If Chad is right, whatever is there predates the horrible, bloody, tragedy of the Battle of Gettysburg.

There are legends which tell of a great Native American battle that occurred in the area. Sometimes called *The Battle of the Crows*, the evidence for this battle is based on, it seems, a great amount of arrowheads and axe heads found in the area.

Local author, Emmanuel Bushman wrote of this possible Native American battle in the *Gettysburg Compiler* newspaper in

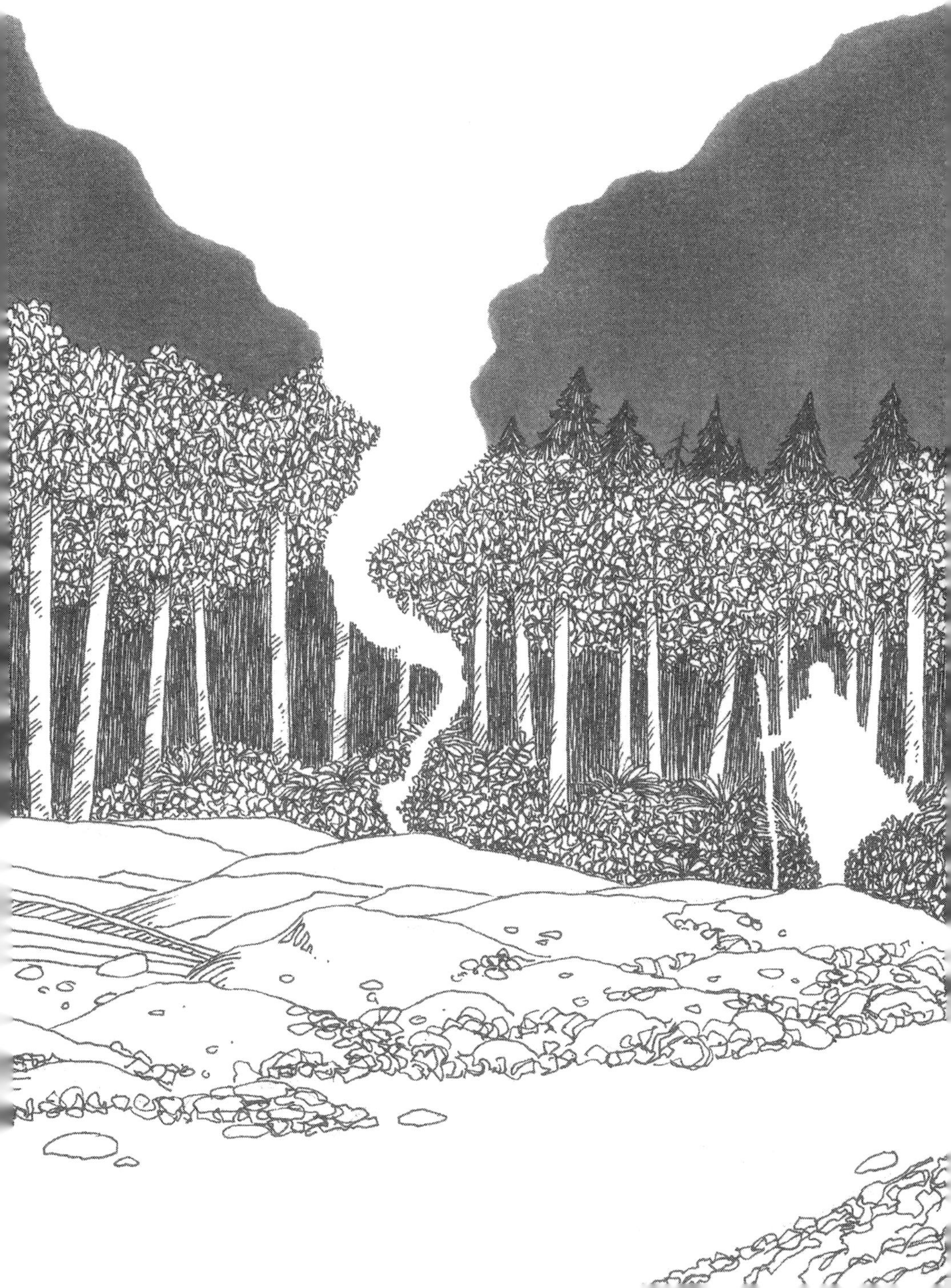

1880. "There is an old Indian tradition of a great battle being fought there," Bushman noted, regarding a place known as the *Indian Fields* near Big Round Top and Devil's Den on the battlefields. He continued, writing "there were Indian arrows, tomahawks, beads, some broken pottery, and fossilized human bones" found at the site. Interestingly, Bushman also wrote that early European settlers had heard "Indian warwhoops" and told "wonderful stories of ghosts and hobgoblins seen there in the still hours of the night."

Was something Other drawn to the region long before the Civil War—and indeed long before the Europeans ever arrived on the shores of North America? If so, why does it stay?

Boundaries

There are natural boundaries in the area, marked by Willoughby Run and Marsh Creek and while these make obstacles of varying difficulty for humans and wildlife, they are not impassible by any means. Even without the two bridges, crossing either creek in normal weather conditions would be more of an inconvenience than a danger.

However, when dealing with the paranormal, the idea of boundaries adds a new twist to our story. In both Old World and New World folklore, there exists the idea that certain supernatural forces cannot cross water, and in particular running water. Countless tales exist of ghosts, revenants, faeries, vampires, and other supernatural entities stranded on one side of a creek, or river, unable to ford even the shallowest depths. On both sides of the Atlantic, different traditions held that the dead should be buried on islands, to keep restless spirits from troubling the living.

Is something Other somehow held or trapped on the land

between the two bridges by Marsh Creek and Willoughby Run?

Another type of supernatural boundary exists as well, at least on the Eisenhower Bridge side—in the form of *iron*. Iron was believed to repel faeries, witches, and ghosts—especially in the form of *cold iron*—i.e. iron worked by human hands. What is Eisenhower bridge but a massive span of cold iron?

While logic might hold that The Other would stay well away from this cold iron structure, we have found that isn't always the case. Iron Furnaces, huge stone towers the ruins of which dot the landscape of Pennsylvania, are often associated with paranormal activity. Could the paranormal be, somehow, both drawn to and repelled by iron? Is the paranormal activity concentrated on Eisenhower Bridge precisely because it represents a barrier which it cannot cross?

There are, of course, other types of boundaries as regards the supernatural—those of a more temporal nature. The first of many knocks we heard at the bridge on our second night occurred just after the sun dropped below the horizon. Night has always gone "bump" with "ghoulies and ghosties and long-leggedy beasties" as the old Scottish prayer notes. Chad visited the bridge several times during the daylight hours to take photographs and survey the surroundings. He noted no creepiness, no cold spots, and no sickness during the day.

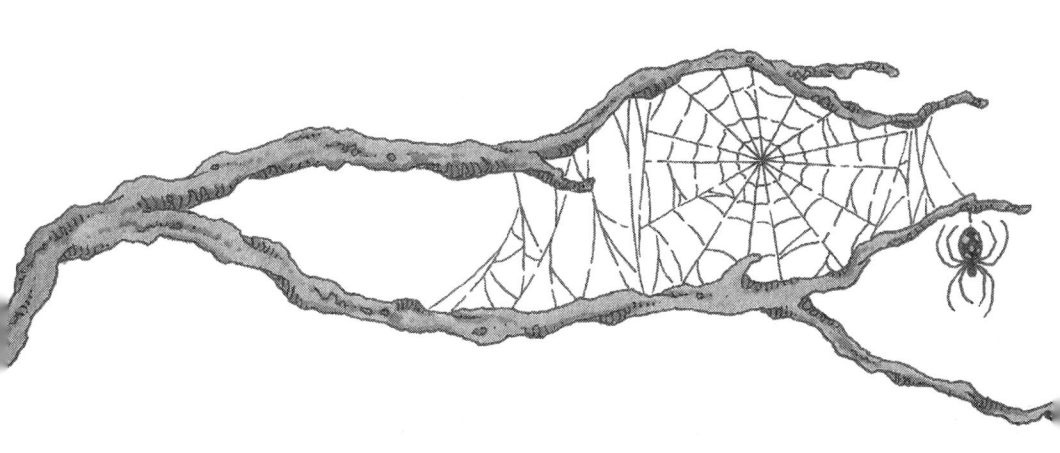

Third Night

It was November 14, 2020 before we returned to the two bridges. As soon as we arrived that evening, as we exited our vehicles, before we even turned on our audio recorders, we were greeted by the sound of a crying baby.

There was no baby we could see and it would be odd for parents to have their infant outside on a cold November night, but it's certainly possible there was a baby somewhere nearby—close enough to hear, but out of sight. On the other hand, John Keel noted that two of the most frequently reported anomalous sounds surrounding paranormal events are those of crying babies and car doors slamming. I had heard the car door slam twice—once on Toad Road and once, deep in the woods along the Susquehanna River, while on a bigfoot investigation with Chad (we actually recorded the car door slam sound on this occasion). Did we hear the supernatural crying baby sound on our third night at the bridges?

We waited on Eisenhower Bridge, wondering what the night would hold. East of the bridge is the Eisenhower National Historic Site (former home of President Eisenhower) and, beyond that, the Gettysburg battlefields. The drive to the Eisenhower Historic Site parallels Red Rock Road. It is lined with trees, which can be seen on the horizon, looking east from the bridge.

A light on the horizon caught my attention. It was swinging as if it were a hand-held lantern and moved, it seemed, from behind one of the trees in a general northward direction. It passed behind another tree as I pointed out the location to Chad. It was possible someone was walking down the drive—though there was something *off* and eerie about the light. The light never emerged from the second tree. If it was a person, they extinguished the light for whatever reason, or else they stayed behind that tree for some time. Still, something struck me as strange about the light.

A thick mist slowly enveloped the area around the bridge. Chad had noted the presence of mist in the area previously, even capturing it on daytime photos when it wasn't present to the naked eye. However, the mist on this night was thicker than we had ever seen. It caused the beams from our headlamps to refract and reflect in ways that caused them to become virtually useless for seeing much beyond our hands.

As much to warm ourselves as for any other reason, we began to walk to Sachs Bridge. As we passed through the dark part of the path, we found the cold spot again—absolutely frigid in the November mist. Chad stated, already, he was not feeling right. "The more I stand here, the more it gets me," Chad complained. "I'm sorry, I don't like it here."

We proceeded down the path, but we hadn't gotten far when a weird cry sounded. It could have been a dog, or a coyote, but there was something *odd* about it. The recording captured two sounds. The first sounds like a dog barking but with some strange audio effect applied or perhaps as if it was played back on a warbled cassette tape (we use digital recorders, so it was not faulty audio tape). The second is lower in tone, possibly a bark but it sounds as if it was issued from a different creature.

Our visit to Sachs was uneventful, so we decided to walk back to the iron bridge. As we approached Eisenhower Bridge, Chad caught sight of a meteor which was immediately followed by an owl hoot.

We returned to our vehicles to warm up for a few minutes. We were parked at the foot of Eisenhower Bridge, where it meets Red Rock Road. After our break, we exited only to be greeted immediately by the sound of a cry (possibly another owl)—which seemed to come from the direction in which I saw the light earlier that night.

Next, we decided to take out the Ghost Box and see what kind of responses we would receive. As we turned on the box and adjusted its various settings, a second cry sounded from the same direction as the previous.

When using the Ghost Box, we apply a sort of modified *Estes Method*. I do not know the origins of this technique. I learned of it through the paranormal documentary series, *Hellier*. This technique involves one person listening in a kind of isolation—headphones are plugged into the Ghost Box and the listener is blindfolded. The listener cannot hear the questions being asked—and only speaks what is heard through the headphones. Likewise, the questioner cannot hear the Ghost Box This creates, in a sense, a *medium* from the listener and creates a kind of separation so, hopefully, neither the person asking questions nor the listener is unduly influenced by the other. (Nor is the questioner influenced by the Ghost Box).

Our modification to the Estes Method involves the lack of a blindfold. We didn't have one on hand, and Chad wasn't particularly keen on being blindfolded on top of Eisenhower Bridge. Instead, I stand behind Chad to ask the questions so he cannot see or hear me. We decided that Chad would be the better medium given his connection and sensitivity to the region.

Given all the issues with Ghost Boxes mentioned in the opening section, the responses we received—and indeed *all* responses from *any* kind of spirit communication—should be taken with a grain of salt. The Other, whatever it is, seems to tell a mixture of truths, half-truths, and outright lies. Folklore and paranormal stories are flush with tales of people squandering their lives looking for buried treasure promised by spirits, or meeting with some kind of unexpected twist when trusting the words of an unseen entity. Likewise, I think that given the Ghost Box as a source for the communication—if there is anything beyond coincidence to it, and The Other is somehow employing the radio to transmit its messages—the medium for communication would be somewhat limited to whatever audible signals were available via the devices at that time. The messages, therefore, might be mere suggestions or truncated versions of whatever The Other is intending to communicate.

With this in mind, we received some very interesting communication on this night. The questions were my own. The replies were Chad, acting as medium, reciting what he heard from the Ghost Box via headphones.

Timothy: Who's here? Or what is here?

Chad: The Other ones striking.

Timothy: Can you tell me anything about who or what you are?

Chad: A gust eventual.

Timothy: What do you have to say to us? What do you want us to know?

Chad: I praise.

Timothy: Is it something to do with the mist here? Can you tell me about Witch Clouds?

Chad: Mastery of today.

Timothy: Come through and let us know about you—about whatever you are.

Chad: Holy...

Timothy: You're holy? Then why do they call this Suicide Bridge?

Chad: Lights in the shadow.

Timothy: There are lights in the shadow—we've seen them...

Chad: I'll be back.

Timothy: Will we see you in the lights or in the shadow?

Chad: Just night. Next time...

Timothy: What about this time?

Chad: Gone away.

We ended this first Ghost Box session. I was somewhat amazed at how many of the replies actually seemed to make sense or address the questions I asked. The first response, "The Other ones striking" (capitalization is obviously my own), seems to address both what we have been calling the collective supernatural—*The Other*—as well as all of the knocks and bangs we heard on and around the iron bridge.

The mention of "lights in the shadow" made quite the impact as well, given the mysterious lights witnessed around the bridge. Likewise, the suggestion that we would see *whatever-it-is* "next time" was prophetic. However, it is the kind of prophecy for which The Other is known: a prediction that leaves the experiencer unsure if what he saw was indeed what the message spoke of—or is the prediction so open-ended and broad (perhaps on purpose), that multiple things could fulfill the augury?

The reply given to my inquiry regarding seeing whatever we were communicating with in the lights or the shadow was very interesting as well. "Just night." Could this refer to the temporal boundaries noted previously?

We turned off the Ghost Box and Chad removed the headphones. Almost immediately we heard voices. "Was that the Ghost Box?" Chad asked. It was turned off. We heard it again. Chad suggested someone else might have a Ghost Box in the area—but where could they be? It would have had to have been at maximum volume—louder than most Ghost Boxes are capable of producing (they are, after all, only modified hand-held radios).

Before long, I caught sight of a red light south of the bridge. It blinked out before I could get Chad's attention. However, it illuminated again and, this time, Chad saw it as well. We headed back down Red Rock Road to try to get a better view.

South of the bridge is a kind of swampy field through which Willoughby Run meanders, roughly parallel to Red Rock Road. Scattered trees and brush dot the landscape. If someone was in the field with a lantern of some sort, or a lit cigarette, we should have seen them. We scanned the area and saw no people. As we stood there, again, we could hear indistinct voices which seemed to come from the direction of the field.

Making our way back toward the bridge, we heard bipedal footsteps which seemed to be pacing us in the field. They were quiet, but audible. Still, we wondered if that was, indeed, what we were hearing until whatever-it-was splashed into Willoughby Run and made three distinct steps in the water. We strained our eyes to see what was walking beside us, but saw nothing in the field.

We have learned, through experience, to check our recorders with some frequency. There have been times, on various paranormal investigations, when the recorders have shut off for no apparent reason. As we headed back to Eisenhower Bridge Chad noticed the red recording indicator light was not lit on his recorder. The batteries had been drained. He had replaced the batteries earlier in the evening. Usually, one set of batteries will last several nights in the recorders we use. It is very unusual that the batteries should have died so soon.

Back at the bridge, we decided to do another Ghost Box session. As soon as Chad placed the headphones on his ears, as if on cue, a light knock or tapping sound issued from the side of the bridge.

We proceeded with the second Ghost Box session:

> **Timothy:** Can you give us some information about you: What you are? What is here? Who is here?
>
> **Chad:** No.
>
> **Timothy:** Ok, why not?
>
> **Chad:** Ain't got...love. So long.
>
> **Timothy:** Does that mean you don't want to talk anymore?
>
> **Chad:** Under bridge.
>
> **Timothy:** What's under the bridge?

Chad: Love, coming.

Timothy: Who are we talking to?

Chad: The man.

Timothy: Ok, do you have a name?

Chad: You're the one.

Timothy: You're talking to me. I'm the one what?

Chad: Rings around me. Let the voice...on one condition.

Timothy: What's that?

Chad: Get out. Run.

During this ghost box session two loud bangs rang out in the distance. One or both could have been gunshots, but as it was now well after midnight, one wonders who is in the area shooting at that time of night? Likewise, it calls to mind all of the reports of the sounds of ghostly gunfire or distant cannon shots heard by witnesses all over the Gettysburg battlefields including, of course, at Sachs Bridge.

The aforementioned vision of manifesting a spirit on the bridge, complete with magic circles, burnt offerings, and all the occult trappings appeared in my mind's eye. This, coupled with the final message from the Ghost Box, "Get out. Run," was enough for me to call it a night.

The Ritual That Never Was

In the days following our third night at Eisenhower Bridge, my mind turned frequently, almost obsessively, to that vision. It was somehow both frightening and enticing. I began, somewhat trepidatiously, preparing myself for the ritual: researching the techniques I might use and talking to friends and associates who practice magic to get their advice and suggestions on going forward with the operation.

The first Ghost Box session at the bridge suggested we would see the entity "next time." The second session brought the vision of the ritual to my mind with the statement, "You're the one... rings around me." Was I supposed to complete the ritual so we could see the being, whatever it may be?

I had, in the past, been involved in the deeper and darker side of the occult—joining various groups with three-letter initials—but I had always decided to, instead, go my own way. My Stone Breath bandmate, Prydwyn, when asked to describe our spiritual path—one which seems confusing and sometimes contradictory to those outside looking in—said, with a simplicity and poetic brilliance that I have never yet been able to match, "Some things hum. Some things do not hum. I follow those things that hum."

So-called "high" occultism never *hummed* for me. There's a kind of complex hierarchy that never appealed to me in that kind of occultism. There were those who "knew"—and those who didn't. Those who had all the special ritual gear—and those who couldn't afford it. Those who owned the obscure and out-of-print books—and those who did not.

I prefer the "folk" approach. It is purer and simpler. Folk magic, like all things folk, is for the people—not the priests or the experts (however they gained that title). I think there is a reason *The*

Long Lost Friend—a book of folk magic, prayers and charms which is the cornerstone of the Pennsylvania *braucherie* or powwow tradition—has been in print consistently since its first publication. *The Long Lost Friend* is for the people. *The Long Lost Friend* simply *hums* for me.

However, I had been given that vision. I thought, for some time, that I must fulfill this premonition. That by *not* casting that magic circle I would be committing an act of cowardice or, worse, not manifesting the future that I was meant to inhabit.

Something else was nagging at me though. Whatever we had been dealing with on this bridge did not seem to be a pleasant entity or group of entities. There is a darkness that hangs over the place. Chad had gotten sick both at the location and directly afterward. He had declared the entity vampiric, and I was beginning to wonder if he was correct.

So, that part of me which distrusts being led—the same part which responds best to the idea and practice of "question everything"—perhaps the same part which is always listening for that *hum*—began to wake up. Casting circles and manifesting spirits—that's not *me*. It's not something I wanted to do. It's something I felt like I *had* to do, based on a vision I had while standing on a haunted bridge. But what if that vision was not my own desire but the desire of something else? Something Other. Something which was trying to lead me down a path upon which I did not want to walk?

As I started to pull away from the idea of performing this ritual, something else occurred to me. As clear as the vision had been, I only saw myself, *alone* on the bridge. Where was Chad in this situation? What was his role? Chad had been with me throughout this experience. He helped me research the historical aspects of the bridges and was right there beside me, boots on the ground, when we visited the locations. Was something trying to separate us? For what purpose?

The moment I decided *not* to do the ritual, it was as if a Witch Cloud lifted from my own shoulders. I felt a kind of clarity settle in, and a new kind of calmness as regards the iron bridge. It is a strange and enticing place, but it would not claim my heart or soul.

Perhaps the "suicide" for which the bridge is named

represents not the loss of life, but instead, manifests in the loss of *self*. A kind of occult/paranormal obsession which can distract one from his true path. It is a symbolic leap, for sure, but as we could find no records of anyone actually taking their lives on the bridge, perhaps there is some weight to the idea.

I wonder, had I drawn that circle upon the bridge, and completed the ritual to manifest whatever is there, would the Witch Cloud have taken some part of me into its dark mist?

Fourth Night

Chad and I visited the two bridges once again on May 1, 2021. It was a mild Saturday night and the ghost hunters were out en masse. My mind was firmly on the Ghost Box message from the previous visit. This visit was "next time." Would we see the entity as promised?

There was a large crowd of ghost hunters at Sachs Bridge. Suitcases of equipment were deployed and those hoping to capture spectral evidence were wandering around with various electronic devices: meters; cameras; smartphone apps which claim to be able to detect the presence of ghosts; and, of course Ghost Boxes.

We made our way to Eisenhower Bridge. A few people would wander over from Sachs but, as noted previously, they never seemed to stay for long. Chad and I would observe several groups come, and leave rather quickly. We recognized two of the men as ghost hunters from the crowd at Sachs. They walked through the darkest part of the path, onto the iron bridge, then immediately turned and started walking back toward Sachs Bridge. We stopped them to ask some questions. Jim and Matt were ghost hunters from Bethlehem, Pennsylvania and Manhattan, New York respectively.

They visited Gettysburg frequently in their quest to find spirits. We recorded the interview on the darkest part of the path, just west of Eisenhower Bridge.

Chad: I just asked you guys 'how long have you stayed here?'—and you said you were just here for a minute and now you're leaving...

Jim: Yep.

Chad:...and you don't know why...correct?

Jim: Yeah.

Matt: Yeah.

Timothy: How did you find out about this bridge? Sachs Bridge is popular—how did you find out about this one?

Jim: Well, we've come down several times...

Matt: Yeah, we heard from a tourist...

Jim: Well, yeah, there was a woman that was on Sachs Bridge that we had spoken to for about half an hour. It was November—it was cold as hell. I just talked to her for about 20, 30 minutes and she happened to mention this bridge and that she was a psychic medium and this was a heavily active area. So we figured, ok, at some point we'll check it out. Tonight seemed like as good a night as any. I don't know why.

Timothy: So, what did she call this bridge?

Jim: Suicide Bridge.

Timothy: Ok.

Chad: How are you feeling right now?

Matt: Fine. No chills, no nothing.

Jim: Oh, I felt something on that bridge.

Matt: I didn't feel anything.

Jim: Actually, I'm just gonna flat out level with you: When I walked onto that bridge it just felt heavy. Mid-bridge I just felt something heavy. No, I mean, whatever I felt over there—I got a chill.

Matt: Actually, it does feel a little cool.

Jim: Another thing, too, I don't know if you saw us walking down here with a flashlight—I kept looking off to the left—because I felt like something was over there walking beside us.

See, he recommended [Jim motioned to someone leading a ghost tour nearby]—I was talking to him on Sachs Bridge—a Necrophonic app or something [a ghost hunting app for smartphones]—and I had that on, and I could hear stuff going crazy while we were walking down here. Like, whispers—and I'm like "Is this the way to the bridge?"—and then I heard something like [in a whispered voice], "yeah."

We proceeded to walk a bit further down the path.

Timothy: Right here's the cold spot. Right where you're standing.

Jim: Yeah, I can feel it.

So, when we hit this point, roughly, was when I felt like something was over there...like off to the left.

Timothy: That tracks.

Chad: That locks in to what we've experienced.

Jim: So you've had that too?

Timothy: Oh yeah.

Jim: Because it felt like a man—like a male figure. I didn't see it, but I definitely felt it and definitely I know it was there. It was right about here where I got that chill and I'm getting it now.

Timothy: The cold spot here...

Jim: Yeah, I feel it.

Matt: [shivering] Whew.

Jim: I feel like I'm in a fridge.

Chad: Did you feel anything else—besides just cold?

Jim: Just like somebody was walking right beside us, following us up to the bridge.

I just saw something...

Chad: There's a light over here that's actually from the house...

Jim: No it's not that. That's not it. I thought I saw something move from over there to, like, where that tree is.

Chad: I believe you.

Matt: All I keep seeing is black shadows...

Jim: Well, that's what I thought I saw—[it] was like a man-ish 6-foot-5, 7-foot whatever-the-heck...dark.

Chad: It's ok. I see it too.

We spent some time looking for whatever Jim and Chad saw, but found nothing.

Chad: Well, thanks guys. Thanks for talking to us.

Jim: Yeah, no problem.

Matt: No problem.

Timothy: Maybe we'll run across you again.

Jim: I'm sure we'll be back. I'm not sure about this bridge. That bridge [Eisenhower Bridge] had a weird—I can't describe that.

...Did you guys hear that? It was like a loud growl I thought I heard.

Chad: Yep, that's typical here.

Jim: Whatever the hell that is—that is not human.

Matt: It just got really cold.

Chad: It wasn't a coyote—I know that for a fact.

Matt: [shivering] Whew.

We said farewell and watched Jim and Matt walk back

toward Sachs Bridge. Later, as I listened to the interview I was able to pick out the growl Jim mentioned. It was audible, even beneath our voices. It did not sound distant at all, but seemed to be very close to the microphone.

It was after midnight and all the ghost hunters had left the area. Chad and I watched from Eisenhower Bridge as the last of the group pulled away, leaving us alone on the dark span. We stood in silence, happy to be able to hear sounds other than people talking, phone apps, beeping meters, or Ghost Boxes. Had there been any owls or knocks before, they would have been difficult to hear over the coming and going of all the ghost hunters.

There were no knocks, this time, nor owls (yet), but we did hear a single tone. It sounded, perhaps, like a tone a car might make—either as a door opening chime, or an alert that one has left the lights on perhaps—but there were no vehicles around us save for Chad's, and that was off with the doors shut and locked. We were the only ones on the bridge at this time.

About 20 minutes later, a car pulled up. A family of three exited—a mother, a father, and a young child—presumably tourists who were checking out some of the local haunted sites. We watched as they walked, holding hands, across the bridge and into the darkness beyond. As the family stepped onto the darkest part of the path a red light crossed directly behind them. It looked as if someone high up in the trees had a laser pointer and shot it across the path behind them. There was no one in the trees.

We were somewhat concerned to see a child being taken into this area, however, we didn't want to scare the family—*especially the youngster*—unnecessarily. If we warned them about things we and others had experienced there, or followed them into the darkness to keep a protective eye on them, we could have frightened them more than anything they might have experienced. It was possible, after all, that *nothing* would happen while they were there. We decided to stay on the bridge, but listen closely in case they should need help.

We did not have to wait long. After only a minute or two, the family of three emerged from the shadows, crossed the bridge, got in their vehicle, and left.

Again, Chad and I had the bridge to ourselves. We talked

quietly, pausing frequently to listen for anything out of the ordinary. About eight minutes into our conversation a low thud sounded nearby. It almost sounded like a car door shutting but there were no vehicles but ours in the area.

At about 1:40 AM, another ghost tour group came and set up their equipment on Eisenhower Bridge. Various meters were deployed as well as a laser grid (set to sound an alarm if any movement breaks the beams), and a Ghost Box was activated. The tour guide mentioned a story involving a distressed husband and father—a man named Andrew—who killed himself on the iron bridge.

Worrying that I might have missed something in my research, I asked the guide, Clinton, for more information on this suicide: a last name; a date; something that might point me to a newspaper article, a death certificate, or *anything* that could confirm this tragedy. He replied that this story, like all the others asserting suicides happened on Eisenhower Bridge, seems to be nothing more than a local legend.

However, as to the veracity of the suicide legends, Clinton said, interestingly:

> Does it matter anymore? It's like, you have this rumor—you know, the story that I've always heard is that there was a gentleman named Andrew who killed himself here. Ok, so this starts the rumors, right? Then you get people who are coming out here and putting all this energy into the place and performing—you know, like working seances and ouija boards... I had a friend who came out here one night and he said that there was a pentagram scrawled out here on this bridge. So, does it matter if what started the rumors were true? Because now they've called things in here.

We swapped some stories about some of our experiences on the bridge. After mentioning the knocks and bangs we had heard there, Clinton added:

> Last week... there was a knock that was so loud back here... it really freaked my guests out. It was like this loud "Pop!", you know?
>
> One night I was here with a guy and he had his five-year-old son. It was a group of about ten of us. Everyone was kind of walking around—doing their own investigations... So, we were standing up here and I heard footsteps. I mean, it was straight up bipedal footsteps down here on the bank and one of them—it cracked a branch, like really loud. This wasn't a squirrel. It was a bipedal *something* with enough weight to crack a branch... So, I had my flashlight—as I always do. I shined my light down here—looked for eyeshine—saw nothing. No eyeshine, nothing. Zero.

Having taken enough of his time, we left Clinton to his ghost tour and turned to leave. As we approached our vehicle we heard a barred owl call, loud and clear. Given what Bethany and Shannon told us regarding owls, and our own experiences with the same, we turned directly around, and walked back onto the iron bridge. Clinton confirmed that, in his experiences on the bridge, the owl calls did seem to precede strange happenings.

The meters Clinton and his tour had brought with them started to register electromagnetic disturbances. The barred owl called several more times.

Clinton continued:

> I guide here, right? I bring people here a couple nights a week. These people come from all over the country. They don't know anything about this bridge... this is local. I'll tell people to just go take a walk down that way [west of the bridge, onto the darkest part of the path]—and I don't say anything more than that—and everyone, they walk about 20, maybe 25 yards, in that direction—and they all,

almost at the exact spot—they get creeped out. They stop. They don't want to go any further. And they all turn around and come back and say,'we feel like we're being watched.'

We stayed with Clinton and his tour for another 40 minutes. The owl calls brought no new strangeness in their wake. It was now almost 3:00 AM and we decided, at last, to pack up and head home, leaving the two bridges behind us once more.

Confirmation

While we experienced some very interesting moments on the bridge during our fourth visit, the most compelling aspect of the night was the confirmation of our own experiences by people we had never met before.

Jim and Matt didn't stay long at Eisenhower Bridge, experienced the cold spot, and simply seemed to want to put the bridge behind them. Clinton, too, mentioned that people he leads on tours to the area walk into the darkness, west of the bridge, then quickly return. Clinton also spoke of hearing knocks on the bridge.

A black, 7-foot tall man-shaped thing was seen. The sound of footsteps just off the path was heard—and Clinton shared a story of heavy bipedal footsteps along the bank of Willoughby Run. A loud, low growl was heard. These things sound as much like bigfoot reports as ghost stories.

What of that black, shadowy figure? Chad saw it, along with Jim. Did this fulfill the Ghost Box prophecy that we would see whatever may be haunting Eisenhower Bridge "next time"? I found it interesting, as well, that Clinton mentioned his friend found a pentagram "scrawled" on the bridge. Had someone else been summoning spirits on the iron span? Was that somehow connected to my vision of the ritual on the bridge?

The Mystery Unsolved

Suicides that never happened. Ghosts of people that never died. Creatures that should not be. Spectral women in white. Mystery lights. Unexplained sounds. Sickly smells. Poltergeist activity.

The truth about any paranormal "investigation" is that there are only two outcomes: either the investigators find a natural explanation for something witnesses previously felt was supernatural; or there is *no* explanation at all. This latter outcome may not be very satisfying to some, but we simply don't know what we are dealing with. We don't know what UFOs or bigfoot really are—and, despite the claim of armies of ghost hunters—we don't really know what ghosts are either. All of these things are simply Other.

There is no explaining or defining The Other, really. It is a wriggling snake, twisting in your hands. Try to pin it down and it will slither away. Sometimes its scales shine with a mysterious beauty. Other times its eyes gleam with a sinister knowledge that it may issue a venomous strike, when least expected.

With all of this in mind, Chad and I don't really seek to *explain* anything. Instead, we place ourselves in these situations—in these haunted areas—to behold The Other, in all its wonder and foreboding. The Other is not a mystery to be solved. It is an experience.

The Witch Cloud still hangs between the haunted bridges, waiting for the next experiencer.

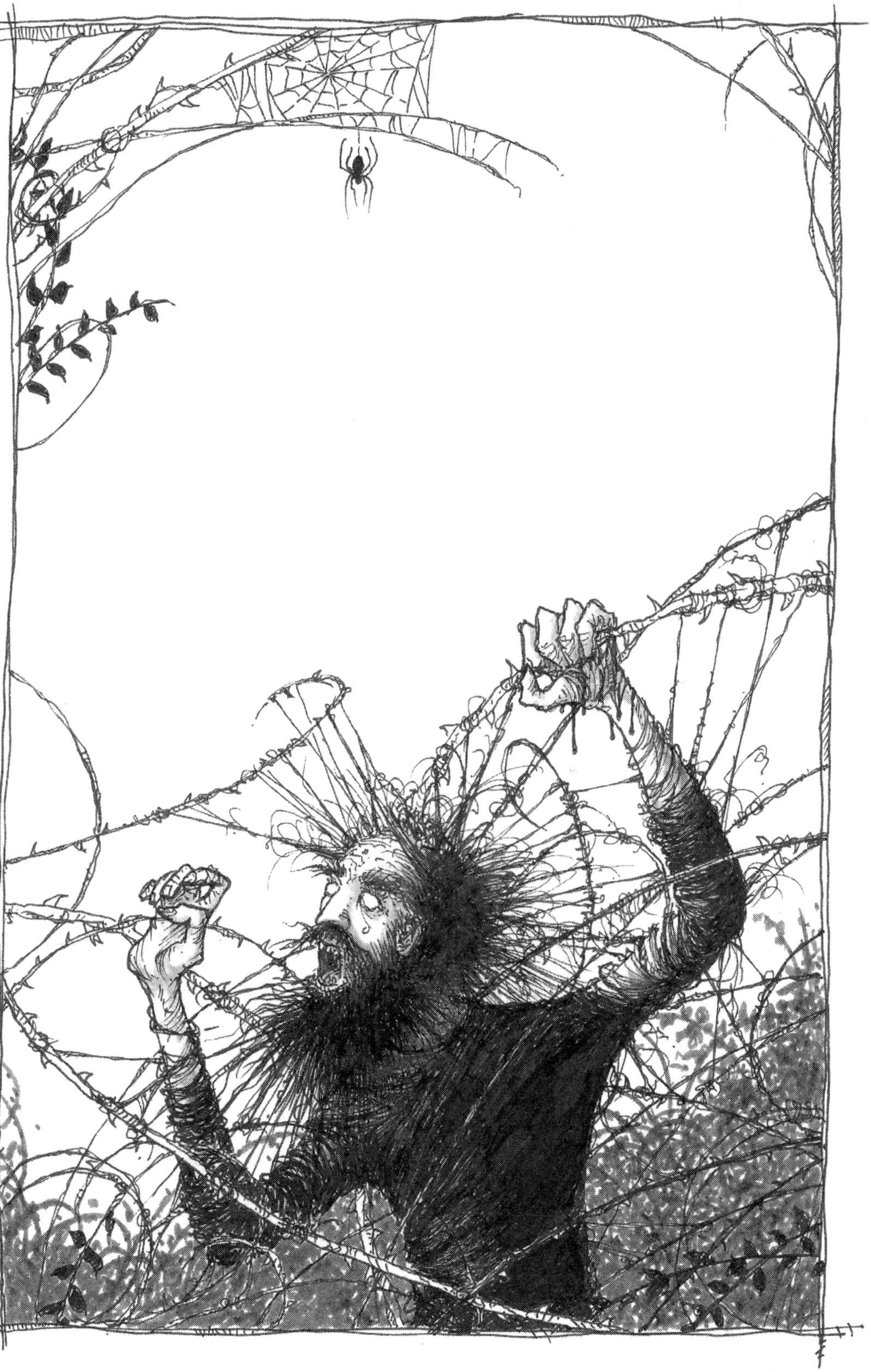

Appendix: The Haunted Bridge on Solomon Road

On Solomon Road, outside of Gettysburg, another haunted bridge spans Rock Creek. Unlike Eisenhower and Sachs bridges, the Solomon Road Bridge is still open to automobile traffic. Legend-trippers and ghost hunters beware: vehicles travel the road and bridge at a considerable speed. There is no sidewalk or pedestrian path on the bridge.

The ghost stories attributed to the Solomon Road Bridge vary, but seem to always involve a woman. Bob and Bonnie Wasel, in their book, *Haunted Gettysburg: Campfire Ghost Stories*, report that the spectre in question was the victim of an automobile accident. According to the Wasels, the accident in question occurred some time before the older bridge was replaced with the current structure in the 1970s. (The Wasels give the date of the new bridge construction as 1972, but my own research suggests the current structure was built in 1977).

The ghostly tale, as given by the Wasels, states that a couple, after having had too much to drink in Gettysburg, crashed their vehicle through the guardrail on the bridge and careened into the bank of Rock Creek. When emergency crews arrived, they found the driver, a man, still in the vehicle, but with such extreme injuries that he could not be saved. The passenger seat was empty.

Searching the scene of the accident, a policeman was greeted with a horrible sight indeed: still grasping part of the guardrail was a woman's arm–the limb having been wrenched from her body as she took hold of the structure when the couple's automobile launched over the side of the bridge. As the story goes, the rest of the woman's body was never found. Presumably it washed down Rock Creek and became lost somewhere in the muddy creek bottom. It is said that this woman's one-armed spirit still roams the area as if it is seeking her lost appendage.

Another story of the Solomon Road Bridge, as told in an online forum, places the origins of the ghost around the time of the Civil War. In this version, the woman was a mother, pushing her baby in a carriage across the bridge–which was a one-lane structure at this time. Somehow, the baby was pushed off the bridge (possibly by a passing horse-drawn cart) and drowned in the creek below. The mother died a short time later (whether she expired from injuries acquired in the accident that killed her child or from grief at the loss of her baby, it is not stated).

The mourning mother's ghost, it is said, still haunts the bridge. According to some legend-trippers, her spirit will push your car if you stop and place it in neutral while in the middle of the bridge. Other lore states that if one utters the phrase "I killed your baby," audible screams will be heard. Some people have reported being scratched by the ghost.

An article on the *Gettysburg is Fun* blog reports that those who desire to experience the ghost on the Solomon Road Bridge, are to park their vehicle in the center of the bridge, turn off the engine and the lights, close the vents, roll up the windows, and wait. An apparition of a woman is supposed to float over the automobile, after which the car will not start. Following this, the car will move and rock as if something is pushing the vehicle.

The author of the blog post reported visiting the bridge multiple times, experiencing the reported engine failure–and the feeling of the car being pushed–more than once. On another occasion the author reported hearing an unexplained knocking sound issue from the vehicle's dashboard. Following this, a "huge beam of light" shone from the nearby woods and into the car. The blog post's author described the events as "one of the most scariest [sic] nights we have ever experienced on Solomon's Bridge."

As with the legends attributed to Gettysburg's other haunted bridges, I did not expect to find any documented news stories to back up the urban legends. Nevertheless, I tried to find anything which might indicate the stories were based in some sort of history.

The original name for the structure was Lott's Bridge. I could find no record of pre-automobile tragedies associated with the span. A few minor auto accidents occurred on or near the bridge, but I could find no reports of casualties and certainly no mention of grisly disembodied arms grasping the guardrails.

A *Gettysburg Times* article published on November 23, 1960 reported that a 49-year old woman named Alizetta Smith was "kicked over" the bridge wall on Solomon Road. She was attacked and robbed by two unidentified men in their twenties. The young men stripped the woman of her clothes and took her purse before pushing her over the bridge and fleeing in their vehicle. Mrs. Smith, however, was not killed in the attack - she only sustained "painful bruises and minor cuts."

The fact that some of the legends suggest that a phrase is to be spoken to the ghostly woman upon the bridge ("I killed your baby") recalls another spooky tale from a very small town called Pond Bank, just west of Gettysburg in Michaux State Forest.

Michaux itself is home to multiple ghost stories and strange encounters–including many, many bigfoot sightings.

Pond Bank has as its namesake, a small pond, which itself is said to be haunted by the spectre of a woman-in-white, known as *The White Lady of Pond Bank*. Legend has it that the White Lady drowned her baby in the pond and is doomed to haunt the area. To summon the White Lady one is supposed to stand at the pond and chant, "White Lady, White Lady, I have your baby." The ghost is then said to appear across the pond.

Not only are the legends of the White Lady of Pond Bank and the ghost of Solomon Bridge similar, but the places share something else in common. Along with the tragic legends of women who have lost their children at both locations, a burial ground named *Pine Bank* is a very short distance from the Solomon Road Bridge. The names *Pond Bank* and *Pine Bank* are so similar, one wonders if it is synchronicity, chance, or perhaps some paranormal word association that connects these two places.

The Pine Bank Cemetery is just east of the Solomon Road span, and back the appropriately named Cemetery Road. This author could find no ghost stories associated with the burial ground; however, an internet search shows various paranormal groups have "investigated" Pine Bank Cemetery. Whether these investigations resulted from reports of paranormal happenings, or were, instead, due to the assumption that cemeteries, by their very nature are haunted, I could not discern.

Nevertheless, Pine Bank Cemetery has an interesting story worth relating. Known as one of the older burial grounds in Adams County, the origins of the cemetery were told by B.F. Macpherson in his "Backgrounds of Adams County" column from the *Gettysburg Times*, published March 19, 1938:

> Did you ever hear the story told regarding the beginning of this cemetery? If you didn't, we will tell you the tale. In one corner of this plot you will find a small stone containing thereon the following inscription: *Here lys ye body of Adam Livingston who departed this life November ye 6th, 1748. Aged 4 years.*
>
> Now, the child, Adam Livingston was the first person buried on this site. According to the story, friends and relatives were taking the body of the little boy

to the Greater Conewago Cemetery for burial. They had come from some rather distant point in York County, and when they came to Rock Creek they found it impossible to cross due to high water. So they buried the body on the rise of a slight hill, and gradually with the passing of the years other people were buried there—and today it is known as Pine Bank Cemetery.

Whether or not Pine Bank Cemetery is haunted, the proximity of a burial ground so close to the Solomon Road Bridge is worth noting.

Other curiosities and strangeness occurred along Rock Creek. A classified advertisement from the *Gettysburg Compiler* on August 14, 1848, shows a stone quarry was located along Rock Creek– perhaps checking the box for "buried treasure theory" (see page 25).

A few miles north of Solomon Road, a hermit named G.F.G.E. Thomas lived on Wolf Hill, just outside of the town of Gettysburg. The hermit Thomas, a German immigrant, came to the Gettysburg area in the late 1880s or early 1890s. He first lived in a rocky cave on Wolf Hill before building a small but impressive cabin just above Rock Creek. G.F.G.E. Thomas was reported in the papers to be the best marksman in Pennsylvania with a bow and arrow.

By 1909, Thomas began showing up in town in an agitated state. He claimed some neighbors had killed his pet cat, and were bothering him nightly. He requested help from the constable, claiming that he would "cast a spell" and "hypnotize" his tormentors, if they did not cease their bothersome activities.

In February of 1909 G.F.G.E. Thomas was found dead, hanging by a thin strap, in his locked cabin. His death was ruled a suicide.

Around Thomas' cabin and on his person, were found several pieces of cardboard on which were written the Latin phrase *In Hoc Signo Vinces*. This phrase, translated as "in this sign you shall conquer" or "in this sign you shall prevail," originates in a vision given to Constantine before a decisive battle (the Latin phrase accompanied an image of a cross). The phrase has been used by Christians since the time of Constantine as a form of exorcism, repelling curses, demons, and the like. The phrase was adapted into folk magic as well as various Christian occult practices, used for both remedy and protection.

In Hoc Signo Vinces, written on several pieces of cardboard

The hermit of Wolf Hill, G.F.G.E. Thomas.

may suggest that Thomas was practicing powwow (a form of Christian folk magic and faith healing with Germanic roots, still in widespread practice in early 1900s Pennsylvania)–or possibly another form of Christian folk magic. Perhaps Thomas' threats to "cast a spell" on his tormentors were not idle words.

Over the next two years, various itinerant people briefly took refuge in Thomas' former home. None stayed for very long. Strange sounds were heard and eerie sights were seen about the cabin, driving away any who thought to stay. Thomas' spectre was said to traverse Wolf Hill nightly.

In February 1911, two years after G.F.G.E. Thomas' death, his cabin burnt to the ground with no one inside. The cause of the fire, which could be seen from the town of Gettysburg, was ruled a mystery. (For much more on G.F.G.E. Thomas–including audio of the author locating the cave in which Thomas first stayed, as well as the foundation of his cabin, his well, and more–listen to Strange Familiars podcast episode 297: *The Hermit of Wolf Hill*.)

On August 29, 1914, The *Adams County News* reported that Rock Creek was responsible for a "great pest of mosquitoes" which was plaguing Gettysburg.

A man named Edward Gilbert was fishing along Rock Creek in April of 1916 when he saw some bones protruding from the ground. Gilbert proceeded to unearth the skeleton of a man–an unknown soldier, presumably killed in the Battle of Gettysburg. The soldier's remains were removed to the National Cemetery in Gettysburg.

Interestingly, Rock Creek eventually joins up with Marsh Creek, just south of Pennsylvania, forming the Monocacy River in Maryland.

Not one to miss a chance to visit a haunted place, and being a bit of a completist, I headed to the Solomon Road Bridge on February 19, 2022. I did not want to miss one of Gettysburg's haunted bridges! Chad, of course, came with me.

It was a frigid, windy night, though the skies above us were clear and filled with stars. First, we parked along the side of the road and walked to the bridge. Standing in the middle, we uttered the horrible phrase that was supposed to bring the ghostly woman, "I killed your baby." Distasteful as it is, we were there for the full experience.

Nothing answered us. I saw something pale and white stirring across the bridge. I thought, for a brief moment, that the

The author, outside of the Wolf Hill Hermit's cave.

spirit was manifesting. Would we see this ghost? No. It was only a wisp of mist. Except for the wind, the night was quiet.

We repeated the experiment in Chad's truck: lights out, engine off. Our results were the same. No replies. No ghosts. No scratches, thumps, or lights from the woods.

This seems like a good place to note that our experience on the Solomon Road Bridge does not discount the experiences of others. It is a very frustrating thing, as someone who documents paranormal experiences (both my own and others'), to read comments from people along the lines of: "Well, I visited that place and nothing happened to *me.*"...or in the case of bigfoot reports: "Well, *I'm a hunter.* I've been in the woods my entire life. I've never seen bigfoot, so it must not exist." These are frustrating arguments, but arguments which do not, as they say, hold water.

Let's remove the element of the paranormal from the statement and simply make it about a natural animal. I have seen coyote in local parks. However, I know many people who visit the same parks often and have not seen the coyote. Just because these people did not see coyote while they were there, does not mean there are no coyote. "Well, I've been there and I didn't see coyote, so they must not exist." Removing the paranormal element from the argument makes it seem a silly statement indeed. Of course coyote exist. Everyone's experience at any particular locale will not be the same.

It is the paranormal which gives weight to the "I was there and nothing happened to me" argument. For the paranormal, by its very nature, is unusual, uncanny, and strange. Many are inclined to disbelieve from the start. It is, in a sense, a confirmation bias–a disinclination to believe in the supernatural–which allows these arguments to flourish.

As noted earlier in the book, the fact that I could find no historical proof of the legends associated with the Solomon Road Bridge, does not mean that people aren't experiencing strange things at this location–perhaps even strange things directly related to those stories which could have started as fiction, but now have become folklore.

Whatever energy years of scary storytelling imbued in that most liminal of places, the bridge; whatever weirdness was carried along Rock Creek beneath it; whatever strangeness radiates from Pine Bank Cemetery down to the bridge; may all combine to create the same kind of heady mix that surrounds Eisenhower Bridge.

Perhaps we just need to spend more time at the Solomon Road Bridge (a dangerous proposition, especially at night, as it is a well-traveled road)–or, perhaps, whatever is at Eisenhower Bridge just resonates with Chad and me more. We are left, as always when dealing with things paranormal, with many questions and few answers.

Afterword

We had no intention of this project becoming a book. I was in the middle of writing a two-volume series on the weirdness that surrounds bigfoot* when we began visiting the haunted bridges in Gettysburg. I didn't have *time* to take on another book.

However, the more we visited, the *stranger* things got. Chad and I realized we had stumbled into something which would be worth our time. We began digging: looking at maps, new and old; pouring through old newspapers; diving into Pennsylvania legends. This is the kind of research we love to do: standing at the crossroads where folklore and history meet the experiences of modern paranormal witnesses.

I was looking for something to make into a special project for Strange Familiars. By our second visit to the bridges, I knew we had found the subject for this project. It evolved, slowly, growing from podcast episode to book to audio book to some combination of all of these. (You may be reading the book minus the audio—or listening without the book—but the original version of this project presented both together).

Being an artist, I, naturally, decided to add illustrations to the project and, as a musician, I wrote some songs on the theme as well. Though it is a relatively thin volume, the project itself kept getting bigger and bigger.

Chad and I have documented many of our experiences in podcast form on Strange Familiars. I told him I would turn some of these adventures into a book someday. Hopefully, this volume is the first of many.

There is no end to these explorations, because there is no solving the puzzle that is The Other. I have been lucky to find some great friends to walk with on these dark and winding paths. Chad was with me, every visit, to the haunted bridges. This project could not have been done without his help, research, and encouragement. Therefore, I'll end with a quote from Chad himself, who asked me, after reading the first draft of this work...

"Where do you want to go next?"

**Where the Footprints End: High Strangeness and the Bigfoot Phenomenon*, volumes I and II, co-authored with Joshua Cutchin.

Bibliography

- *Adams County News.* No title. Gettysburg, Pennsylvania. August 29, 1914 - page 6.

- *Altoona Tribune.* "This Morning's Comment". Altoona, Pennsylvania. March 20, 1939 - page 4.

- Bigfoot Field Researchers Organization - http://www.bfro.net

    Report 12951: http://www.bfro.net/GDB/show_report.asp?id=12951

    Report 3360: http://www.bfro.net/GDB/show_report.asp?id=3360

- Civil War Ghosts "Sachs Covered Bridge". https://civilwarghosts.com/sachs-covered-bridge/

- The Company Q Dispatches. "Big Round Top and Devil's Den at Gettysburg - Site of Ancient War Between Indian Tribes?" http://companyqdispatches.blogspot.com/2013/04/big-round-top-devils-den-at-gettysburg.html

- Cutchin, Joshua and Timothy Renner.

    Where the Footprints End, High Strangeness and the Bigfoot Phenomenon, Volume I: Folklore. Dark Holler Arts, Red Lion, PA, 2020.

    Where the Footprints End, High Strangeness and the Bigfoot Phenomenon, Volume II: Evidence. Dark Holler Arts, Red Lion, PA, 2020.

- Destination Gettysburg "Sach's Covered Bridge". https://destinationgettysburg.com/members/sachs-covered-bridge/ - retrieved April 5, 2021.

- *Gettysburg Compiler.*

    Classified advertisement "Stone Quarry". Gettysburg, Pennsylvania. August 14, 1848 - page 3.

    "The Indian Field". Gettysburg, Pennsylvania. January 29, 1880 - page 1.

    "Gettysburg". Gettysburg, Pennsylvania. July 18, 1899 - page 2.

    "Gipsy Band Get License". Gettysburg, Pennsylvania. August 31, 1910 - page 1.

- *Gettysburg Daily.* "Willoughby Run Quarry". https://www.gettysburgdaily.com/willoughby-run-quarry/

- Gettysburg is Fun "How to Spot a Ghost in Gettysburg!" https://gettysburgisfun.wordpress.com/2011/12/08/how-to-spot-a-ghost-in-gettysburg/

- *Gettysburg Times.*

    "Finds Bones". Gettysburg, Pennsylvania. April 14, 1916 - page 1.

    "The Meanest Trick". Gettysburg, Pennsylvania. October 16, 1916 - page 1.

    "Truck Crashes Through Bridge". Gettysburg, Pennsylvania. April 26, 1919 - page 1.

    "Cider With Kick Caused Wreck". Gettysburg, Pennsylvania. January 10, 1920 - page 1.

"Rider Thrown 16 Feet in Accident". Gettysburg, Pennsylvania. October 16, 1923 - page 1.

No title. Gettysburg, Pennsylvania. October 15, 1924 - page 1.

"Backgrounds of Adams County No. 32 - Just Rambling" by B.F. Macpherson. Gettysburg, Pennsylvania. March 19, 1938 - page 4.

"Seek Pair Who Beat, Robbed Local Woman Monday Night". Gettysburg, Pennsylvania. November 23, 1960 - page 1.

"Old Bridge Site to be Passive Park" by H. William Sacks. Gettysburg, Pennsylvania. November 7, 1992 - page 1

- Hall, Robert L. "Ghosts, Water Barriers, Corn, and Sacred Enclosures in the Eastern Woodlands." *American Antiquity*, vol. 41, no. 3, 1976, pp. 360–364.

- *Harrisburg Telegraph*.

    No title. Harrisburg, Pennsylvania. August 26, 1910 - page 6.

    "Robber Causes Break of Eggs". Harrisburg, Pennsylvania. June 18, 1919 - page 2.

- Newman, Rich. *Haunted Bridges*. Llewellyn Publications. Woodbury, MN. 2016.

- PA Bigfoot Encounters - Google Maps https://www.google.com/maps/d/u/0/viewer?mid=1YM1KNTl1F18yPhzWzTlg9gciPuU&ll=40.50130696585405%2C-95.6600765&z=4

- Reddit.com/r/paranormal. https://www.reddit.com/r/Paranormal/comments/2e0hgk solomons_bridge_on_solomons_rd_gettysburg_pa/

- Renner, Timothy.

    Beyond the Seventh Gate. Dark Holler Arts. Red Lion, PA. 2016.

    Bigfoot in Pennsylvania. Dark Holler Arts. Red Lion, PA. 2017.

    Don't Look Behind You. Dark Holler Arts. Red Lion, PA. 2018.

- Strange Familiars podcast.

    Episode 15: *Kelly, Don't Pet the Devil Monkey.* August 31, 2017. StrangeFamiliars.com

    Episode 297: *The Hermit of Wolf Hill.* February 24, 2022. StrangeFamiliars.com

- Traditional Scottish prayer:

    From ghoulies and ghosties
    And long-leggedy beasties
    And things that go bump in the night,
    Good Lord, deliver us!

- Wasel, Bob and Bonnie. *Haunted Gettysburg: Campfire Ghost Stories.* Self-published. Gettysburg, PA. 2005.

About the Author

Timothy Renner is an illustrator, author, and folk musician living in Pennsylvania. His illustrations have appeared in the pages of various books, magazines, fanzines and comics as well as on many record and CD covers. Since 1995, Timothy has been making music both solo and with his band, Stone Breath. Timothy is the creator of "Strange Familiars", a podcast concerning the paranormal, weird history, folklore and the occult. He makes regular appearances on the paranormal radio show, "Where Did the Road Go?", and has appeared as a guest on many other podcasts and radio programs, including "Coast to Coast AM".

Books by Timothy:

Beyond the Seventh Gate (2016)
Bigfoot in Pennsylvania (2017)
Bigfoot: West Coast Wild Men (2018)
Don't Look Behind You (2018)
Apparitions: Illustrations of The Other (2020)

With co-author, Joshua Cutchin:

Where the Footprints End, volume I (2020)
Where the Footprints End, volume II (2020)

Photo of the author by Alison Renner

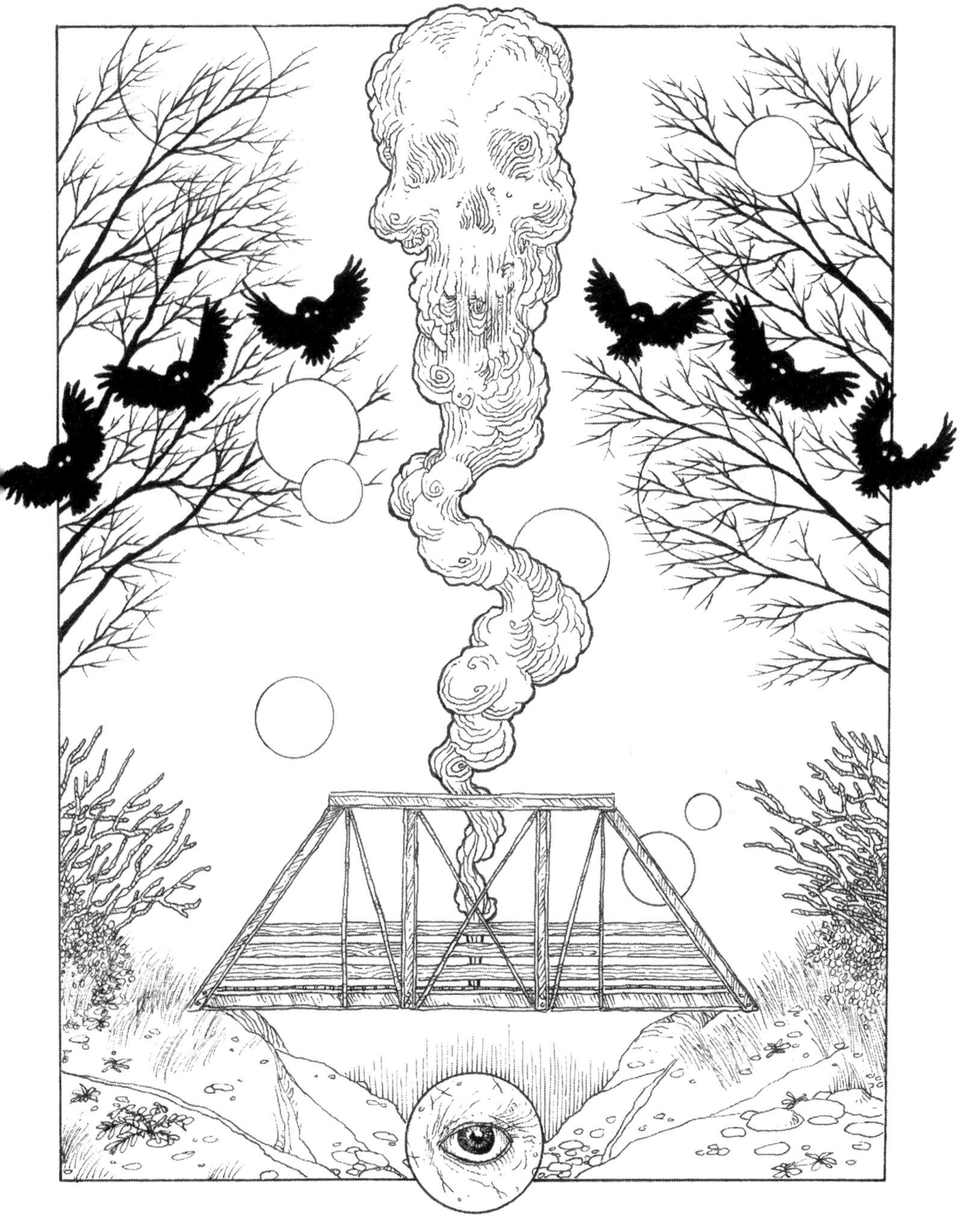

The Witch Cloud was originally published as a hardcover book / audio download in 2021. This multimedia project served as *Strange Familiars* podcast episode 300.

The audio consists of the author reading the text from this book. When possible, the actual recordings of witnesses are used, in lieu of reading the transcription. Likewise, if sounds discussed in the text were caught on the recordings, those sounds were inserted into the audio.

The author, along with his friend and Black Happy Day bandmate, Tara Vanflower, recorded a new song, *Into the Witch Cloud*, specifically for this project.

On October 9, 2021, the author revisited Sachs and Eisenhower bridges, along with Chad and Seriah Azkath of the *Where Did the Road Go?* podcast. This visit was recorded and became a bonus podcast–part of *The Witch Cloud* audio.

Those interested in hearing the audio book/podcast/music can purchase the download at:

https://stonebreath.bandcamp.com/album/the-witch-cloud

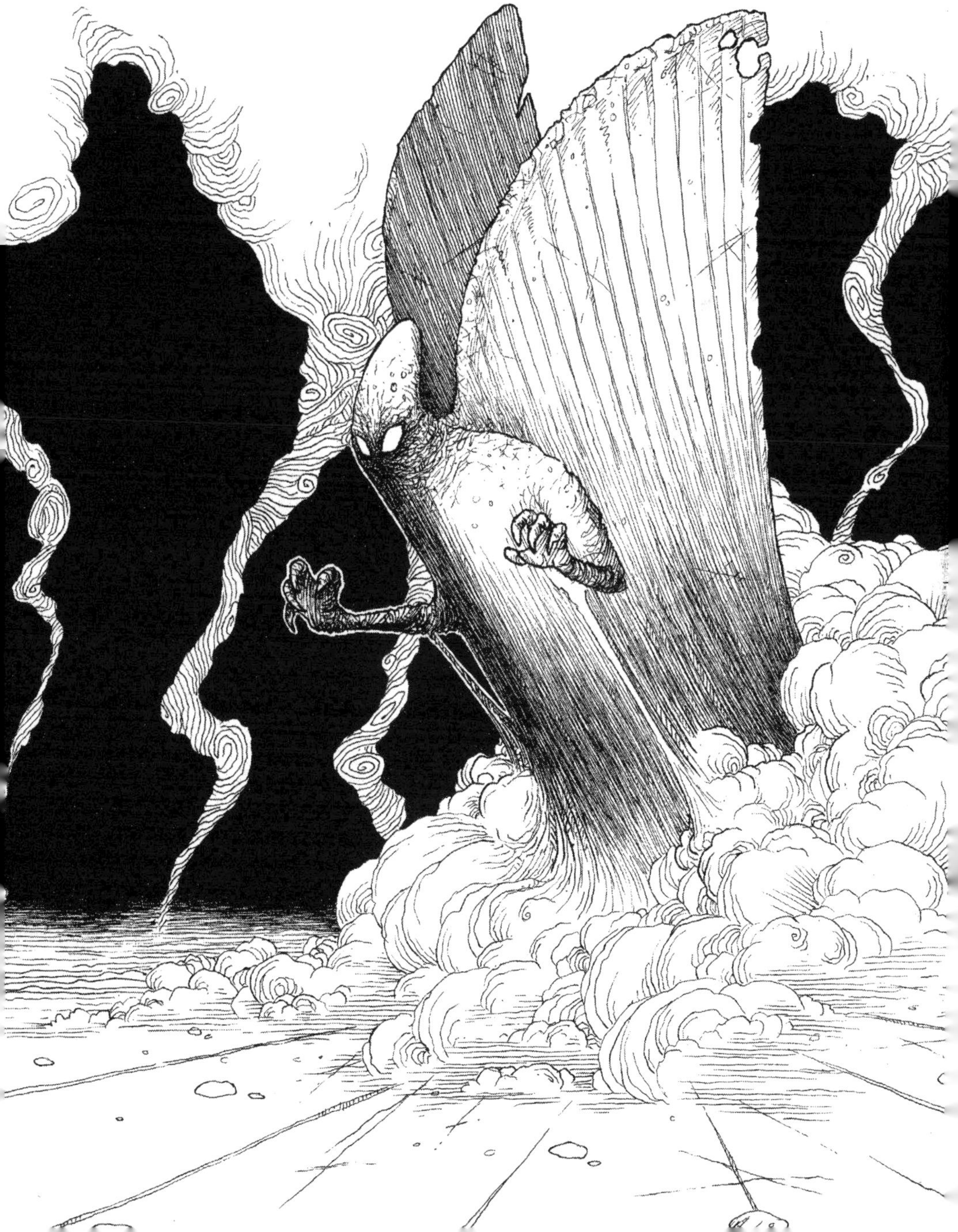

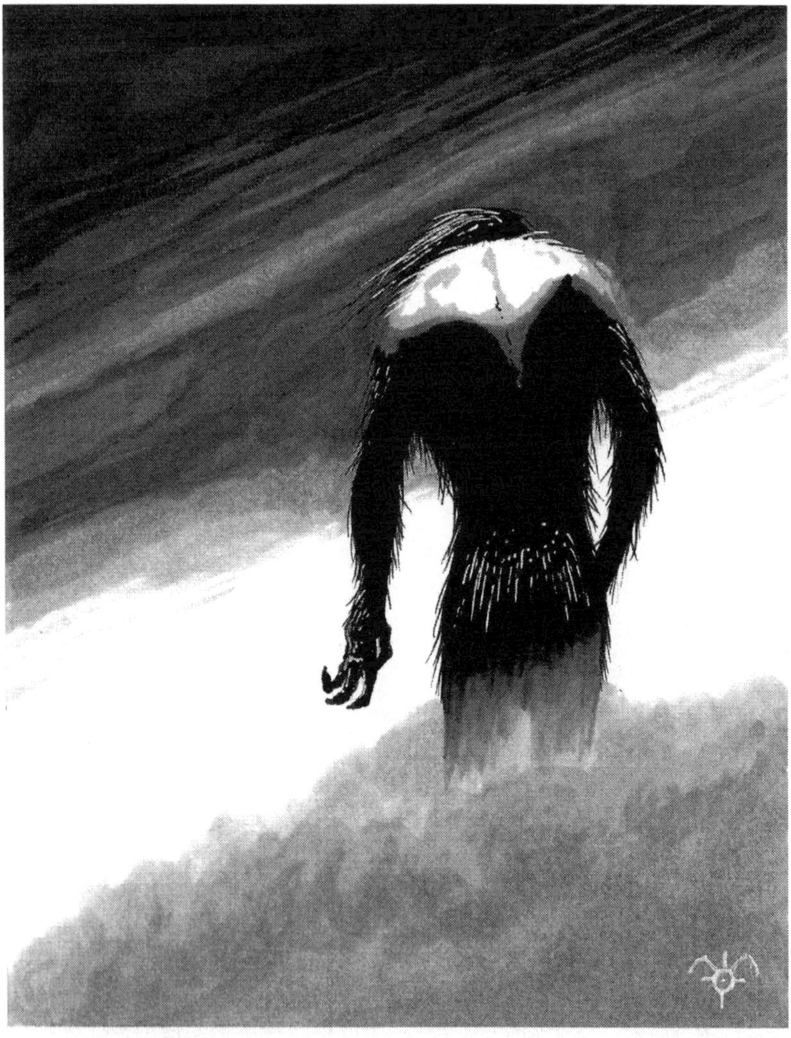

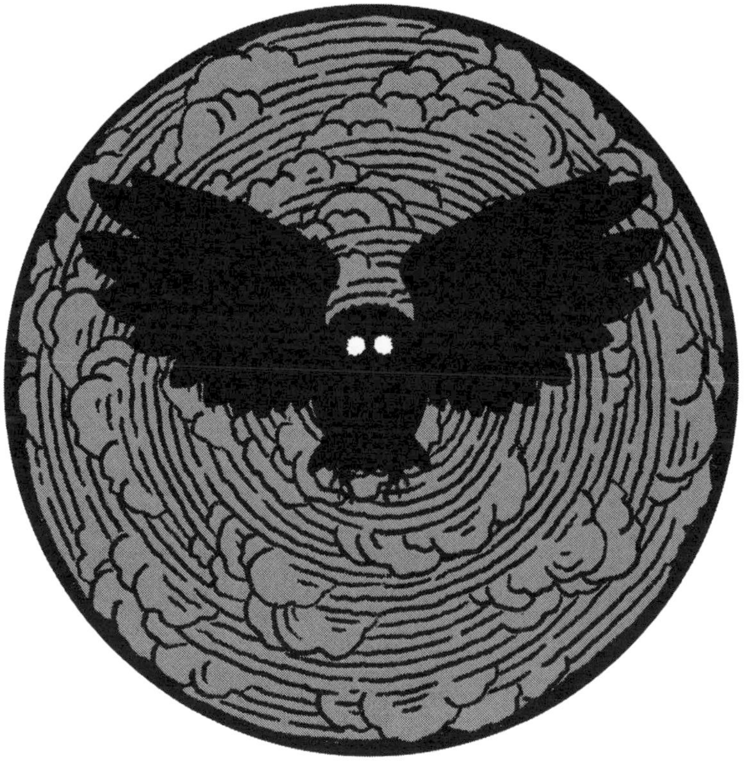

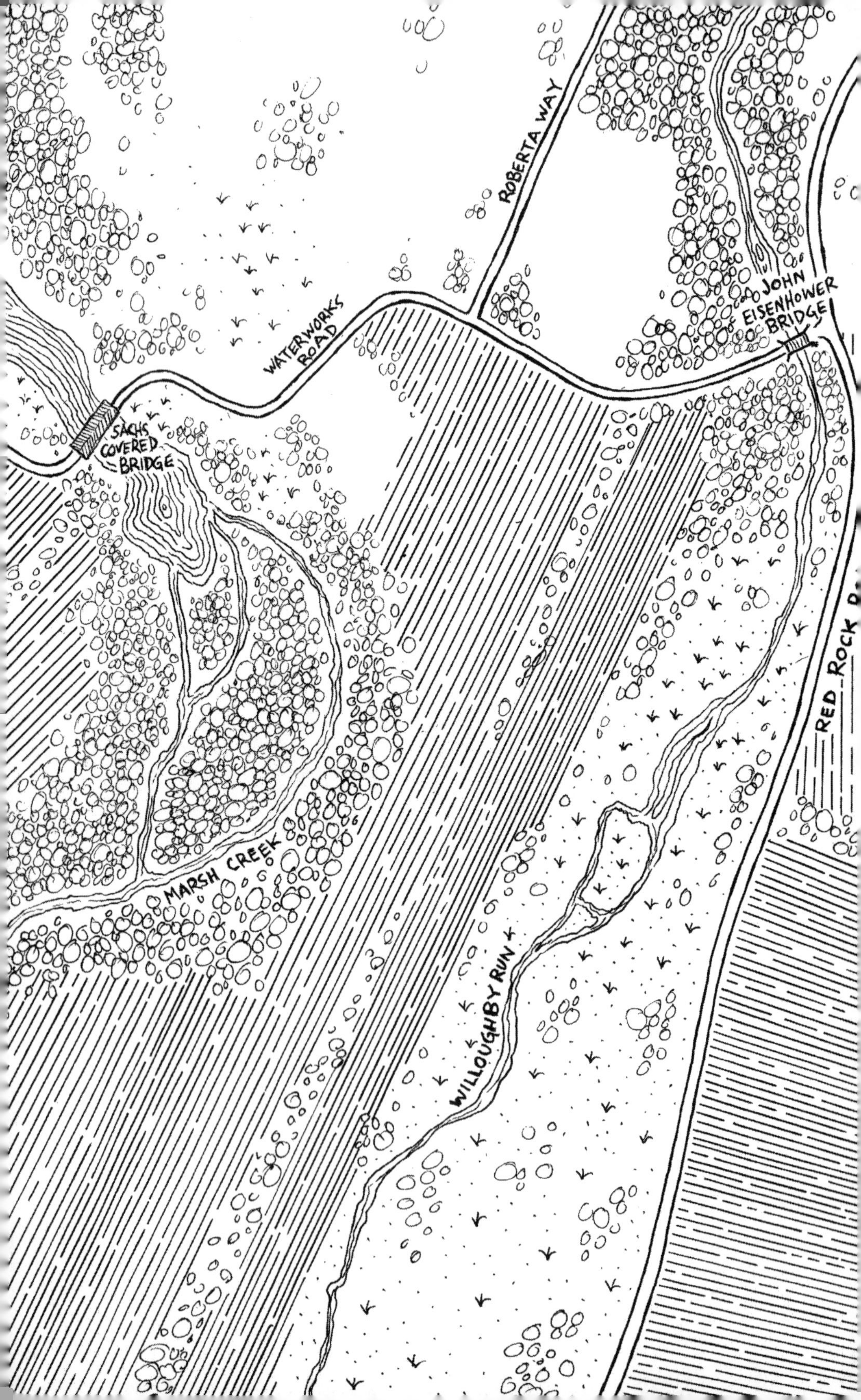
ROBERTA WAY
JOHN EISENHOWER BRIDGE
WATERWORKS ROAD
SACHS COVERED BRIDGE
MARSH CREEK
WILLOUGHBY RUN
RED ROCK

Printed in Great Britain
by Amazon